Made in the USA
Lexington, KY
21 April 2015

Dear Kim,
I have really enjoyed getting to know you these past few months. Thank you for welcoming me to Indianapolis! Enjoy reading your "special" copy of this book! :)
[illegible]

Soul Destination

8 Paths to Balance, Consciousness, Inspiration & Freedom

Soul Destination

8 Paths to Balance, Consciousness, Inspiration and Freedom

The content of this book is for general instruction only. Each person's physical, emotional, and spiritual condition is unique. The instruction in this book is not intended to replace or interrupt the reader's relationship with a physician or other professional. Please consult your doctor for matters pertaining to your specific health and diet.

To contact the publisher, visit
www.CreateSpace.com

To contact the author, visit
www.bellybrain.org

ISBN-13: 978-1507632321
ISBN-10: 1507632320
Printed in the United States of America

Table of Contents

Dedication

For Lee "Granddad" Malins and my grandparents, whose lives have inspired me to live my truth each day.

Acknowledgements

My gratitude for Sarah Diedrick -- fellow health coach, writer, talented yoga instructor, ritual-maker, friend and "wild woman" -- has boundless depth. She was the main content editor of this book and gave me many great ideas that helped it take its current shape. Our weekly meetings kept me authentic, challenged, and inspired.

I also give thanks to my mother, whose eagle eyes and penchant for perfect grammar, syntax and punctuation served as the proofreader for the final copy of the book.

I am eternally indebted to Joshua Rosenthal and the Institute of Integrative Nutrition for making my Path of Dharma so much clearer.

I appreciate the many friends on Facebook who took the time to respond to my posts, and my past and current clients, whose stories gave me additional inspiration.

Last, but far from least, I thank my husband for his honest feedback about each chapter, assistance with the cover design, and his constant encouragement. His patience and support enabled me the time and resources to complete this daunting task.

Introduction ~ How I Found My Soul

This book was never intended to be read by others. It was born at around 3 A.M., birthed by an overworked, overstressed mind and a wrecked digestive system that made sleep impossible on many nights. Yet this particular night, instead of feeling frustrated and stressed knowing that I would not fall back asleep for another two to three hours, I felt a surge of creativity. It's as if a gentle light within me was finally revealing itself in the darkness. Like a lantern, it lit up paths of possibilities that would give me what I craved: a balanced mind, fulfillment in my line of work, days that were infused with creativity and inspiration, and a life of freedom.

In the darkness, as I listened to its shy whisper, I realized I could connect with this internal light every moment by consciously walking these "paths" that would keep me balanced, healthy and present. They had been there all along, but I'd been blinded to them by the distractions of stress and anxiety. The challenge would be to stay on the paths, rather than getting caught in the brambles, so I decided to write down everything I knew that would lead me back to the light of the soul. There was no destination I had to strive to reach, because the destination was a part of me, and it was available to me all of the time. All I had to do was stay awake to the present moment, let go, and have the courage to be authentic.

It's so simple, but far from easy. Otherwise, we'd all be doing it. Most of us are forever making lists, planning for the future, daydreaming about the desired textures and shapes we want our lives to take . . . someday. At that time, I had a job that

would have made any parent proud, with a good salary, respected position, and a noble cause. I should have felt on top of the world, but instead, I felt trampled beneath it. Although I was good at my job, and my happy clients and annual pay increases proved it, I was not living according to my core values. In other words, I was not being authentic.

I knew that in this situation, being authentic meant I had to answer a different calling, leaving behind a world in which I was successful to enter the unknown. It would have been much easier, in some ways, to stay stuck, but I was sick and tired of being sick and tired. I knew I wanted to be inspired, fulfilled and free every day, every moment. I had a hunger that could only be satisfied by returning to my spirit and setting it free. To do this, I had to live according to its true nature rather than grasping for what lay outside me, or allowing myself to be shaped according to someone else's vision.

In seeking to heal myself, I had attended numerous yoga classes, silent meditation retreats, personal development workshops, and wellness conferences over the past 20 years. I had sat at the feet of enlightened gurus and studied the spiritual texts of several religions. I had read books on psychology and self-help. I had learned breathing techniques, meditation tools, tricks for unleashing my creativity, and tips for tapping into my divinity. I had learned to dance like a dervish from a Sufi mystic. Buddhist monks and nuns had taught me how to quiet my mind by focusing on my breath. The Christians had taught me forgiveness by loving my enemies and treating others as I wanted to be treated. I had learned to deepen my relationship with nature, and therefore the divine, through the examples of the Native Americans and

the Druids. The Hindus had given me a sense of community and taught me how to integrate all of the aspects of a spiritual life, from the physical postures of yoga to eating for my constitution. These experiences led to a variety of spiritual epiphanies, a much calmer disposition, and increased mental strength.

And then I slowly stopped practicing the techniques. I fell back into old patterns. Life happened. I got caught up in the day-to-day hamster wheel of working, paying bills, worrying about various family members, dealing with health issues, working for companies where I felt forced into an unnatural mold, and other life challenges. My sleep suffered greatly. During that particular middle-of-the-night awakening, under the gentle light of my soul, I wrote down all of the wonderful tools and tips I had learned over the years that had been effective in bringing my mind to a state of calm. Putting it in book form appealed to the bookworm in me. I enjoy learning from books, and this book would serve as a constant reference for what I should be doing and how I should be living. It was to be a reminder of all of the things I'd tried over the years that had worked, but that I didn't always remember to do. I would do these things, I vowed, if I had all of the information in one, easy-to-locate place rather than in the various spiral notebooks and scraps of notes in my closet or in the remote, dusty corners of my brain.

As I started writing, I had an idea: I should share this with *you*. By putting it down on paper and in a more organized format, I could not only keep myself on track, but perhaps spare you some of the suffering I had endured. In other words, I did not write this handbook because I am some kind of enlightened being who has it all figured out and is now

sharing this with my humble followers. I wrote it because I am deeply flawed and have suffered because of it. I am not standing triumphantly at the top of a mountain, calling to everyone below. I am constantly walking the paths back to my soul and sometimes stumbling down them, half-blind, with leaves in my hair and snot running down my nose. But if I can share what I have learned through my suffering and enable you to travel through life with more ease as a result, then perhaps my purpose on this earth is to share my little flashlight with you as we walk through the tangled thickets of the dark forest together on our circular journey back home to the present, our authentic self, our true nature, the beautiful garden of our soul destination.

This book will provide stories and theoretical understanding combined with hands-on, practical techniques that you can use regularly to continuously awaken to the truth of the present moment and to feel free now rather than later. It is during the present that you begin to understand the gifts you were destined to share and to have the courage to share them. Life becomes richer and fuller. Freedom unfolds, allowing you to break free of the fetters of anxiety that have held you prisoner.

This handbook is yours. It does not need to be read from start to finish, although I would recommend reading all of it eventually. I am not going to quiz you at the end. There are no tests other than those you choose yourself. Scan the chapters and subheadings to see what calls to you. Use this handbook often. Dog-ear the pages. Highlight ideas or phrases that stand out to you. Check out the references listed at the end of the book. There are so many great teachers out there, and I am grateful to all of them. Pick one of these

subsections to delve into for the next week or month or however long it takes for you to notice healing occurring. You don't need to start with the first one. This isn't about structure, but about meeting whatever needs you have in the moment. As much as we would like to apply structure to ourselves and to life, all is fluid and ever-changing. You will notice that the paths overlap since a spiritual lifestyle cannot fully be parceled into chapters. They all intertwine and move through each other. The mind is linear, but the spirit is not. Honor fluidity in yourself and others. Every day is a new day, a new you, and a new everyone else. What you do unto others, you do unto yourself. Life is an intricate web, and the smallest movement affects the entire web. What you do right now *matters*.

As I sit here writing, the leaves outside my window are in full fall color: deep ruby and fiery yellow. Leaves become most beautiful when they change and commit to letting go, dying to be born again. I envision this journey as a walk on the many interconnected paths through a mysterious wooded area in autumn: a time for change, for letting go. There are many paths that lead to the healing power within us, and they all offer a variety of vistas that allow us to see life in a new way. The way you walk the paths that lead back to your soul are unique to you and will change according to the day and moment. Life is not static. Instead, it is a dynamic state of flux, of ebb and flow, of issuing forth and returning.

Come walk with me.

Chapter 1

The Druid's Path ~ Ground Yourself in Nature

"The breeze at dawn has secrets to tell you. Don't go back to sleep."
~ Rumi

"You must learn to become invisible and melt into the air like morning mist." ~ from The Way of Wyrd

The Druids of the ancient Celtic world have long held the fascination of many students of English literature, historians, and those on a quest to commune with the divinity in the natural world. Very little is known about them, as few documents about the Druids survived after the fall of the Roman Empire. We do know that they lived in France, Ireland and Britain. They worshiped in forest groves, held nature to be sacred, and were described as poets, philosophers and wizards. The name Druid means "wise one of the oaks."

I grew up on fifty-six acres that consisted largely of wooded land. Although I envied people who lived exciting lives in cities, I realize how lucky I was to have been raised by nature. Among my greatest teachers were plants and animals of the natural world, and some of my most profound epiphanies occurred in solitude among the trees and wildlife. There is a large, old oak tree on the edge of that woodland. I would often sit beneath its branches to think. I was drawn to that particular tree for whatever reason, and it became like a friend to me, bringing me comfort and insight.

Nature has always spoken to me, whether in subtle ways, like an almost imperceptible whisper, or through profound insight that appeared like a flash of lightning in my mind. One day

when I was younger, I refused to go to church with my family because I saw nature as my church and I felt compelled to spend my time there instead. I sat beneath my oak tree and played my cedar flute, entering into a somewhat meditative state. As I played, the world around me changed. The scenery contained all of the same elements. The trees and the corn field surrounded by a fence were still there, but the world looked watery and dream-like, as if I could walk into another dimension to a different reality. Afraid, I pulled myself back and just sat in awe, unsure if my mind had played a trick on me or if I had arrived at the brink of a profound spiritual experience.

As incidents such as this one faded into the recesses of my mind like a dream, nature would eventually reach out to me again, sometimes in the depths of deepest despair. In my mid-twenties, I found a growth on my thyroid and had it aspirated to determine if it was benign or cancerous. The week I waited to get my results was the longest week of my life. I had no health insurance and was about to go to graduate school in England. A diagnosis of cancer would have thrown me into more debt than I ever would have ever been able to pay off and would have robbed me of this opportunity to study abroad. Then again, I thought, perhaps I should go to England anyway. Since they had socialized medicine there, at least I could afford the medical care.

The waiting became too much to bear, so at dusk one evening, I took a walk through the woods until I found myself in the middle of my grandma's cornfield. The sun had almost completely disappeared behind the hills, leaving me in a mysterious world of light and shadow. I prayed for a sign, any sign, to let me know if I was going to be okay. A moment

later, a large stag appeared at the top of a hill about fifty meters away. He just looked at me, and I at him, for what seemed to be a long time. Slowly, he walked away, and I knew this was my sign. I would be okay. And I was – the growth was benign.

Spending time in nature is essential for everyone. It brings to light the trivial nature of many of our thoughts and the details on which we expend energy, allowing us to take in the majesty and mystery of the natural world around us. Nature connects us to our ancestry, gives us glimpses of the true nature of reality, and teaches us about the spiritual aspects of life. We become part of a magical world that we pass by without noticing.

If we can follow the example of the Druids by learning to connect with nature, we too can receive its wisdom. Suddenly, the oak tree that we rush by on our way to work becomes a wise teacher. The forest becomes a playground, and its plants become our healers. It is a fascinating world teeming with life. It awakens our spirit and brings us into unity with the world around us. Rather than being separate from nature, we realize we are part of it and it is part of us, and the lines of separation dissolve. We belong to an intricate web that connects all in the universe, and each individual action affects the entire web.

Be present

Being present seems like an impossible task for the person who has several thoughts flying around at once in various directions. This is the nature of the world in which we live. It can be hard to focus on the now when we feel the constant pull of the "what's next?" Spend time alone in nature each

week. Jogging down a path with your headphones on doesn't count. Find a rock in a forest or sit very still in a remote corner of a park. What do you notice? Can you identify the smells and sounds you are sensing? Take your shoes off and connect with the earth. Your roots are here, not in a high-rise building. Let your worries drain away, like rain water dripping off the leaves of a tree to be absorbed by the earth.

At first, the slow pace of this experience may seem boring, and you might feel an itch to go back to your home or office to get things done. But if you practice this regularly, you will find an inner calm you didn't know existed. Start with twenty minutes per week. If that sounds like too much, then start with the amount you think you can do, and gradually increase the time. During the cold winter seasons, I wear multiple layers and find a sheltered area from which to observe nature. Although I often dread stepping out into the cold, I am always grateful for the crisp, fresh air in my lungs after days of breathing heated, re-circulated indoor air.

Nature's classroom

Go for a long hike alone or with a friend. A longer amount of time in nature gives additional perspective and allows you to learn much more. Consider nature your classroom. Allow it to teach you as you walk through its groves, thickets and meadows. Avoid spending time chatting about events that have nothing to do with the present moment, turn your cell phone off, and allow nature to teach you her secrets. Listen to the sound of the leaves and twigs under your feet. Observe how and where the various plants grow. Notice the creatures that inhabit the area. Spend time next to a stream or beneath a tree. What do you notice that you didn't notice while walking? Find as many different-colored rocks as possible.

When you go home, find out what types of rocks they are, what elements compose them, and how they are used. You might find some interesting historical facts about how our ancestors used them, as well as how they are used today.

For even more time in nature, go camping in an area that also has great places to hike. Cook your food over an open fire. Learn about edible plants and berries, and then go foraging. What can the forest offer that you can add to your dinner that night? Plan at least one big nature trip per year. Hike part of the Appalachian Trail, visit Yellowstone Park, stroll along the beautiful beaches of Vietnam, cycle along the Amalfi coast, go horseback riding in Mongolia, or walk through the rolling, green hills of the English countryside.

Honor the healing power of trees

Trees are revered in nearly every spiritual tradition. One of the asanas in yoga is called the "Tree Pose," which involves rooting your feet into the ground while stretching your arms towards the heavens. Trees are wonderful examples of what we should aspire towards as spiritual beings temporarily in a human body. Rooted to the earth, trees absorb nutrients from the ground and then give back to the earth by enriching the soil. They also have an airy, spiritual aspect. Their branches extend out and up into the atmosphere, taking in energy from the sun and exhaling oxygen that the animal kingdom inhales. Trees remind us to be connected to earth and heaven at the same time, allowing us to live in a balanced state between the physical and spiritual worlds. Like the tree, we can be the meeting place of both of these realms. This reflects the concept of "Spirit in everything and everything in Spirit."

Trees were so revered by the Celtic world that they inspired a

language. Ogham is an ancient Irish alphabet that was carved onto trees and stones, dating back to Pagan times. It contains twenty-five letters consisting of tally marks, and the inscriptions are to be read from bottom to top. The symbolism contained in each letter is what makes it interesting. Each letter, or "few," is linked to a specific tree, such as the birch tree, and each tree has spiritual meaning attached to it. Birch represents purification and new beginnings. The "elemental attribution" is the "spirit of air." The Ogham alphabet is, in other words, the alphabet of trees. In ancient Druid tree lore, birch was considered to have protective qualities, and so a broom made of birch was helpful in driving out spirits from the previous year. Even today, birch is used for its healing powers, and there are numerous articles about the variety of ways it is used in medicine. For example, birch helps with ailments such as gout and rheumatism, and aids in detoxification overall. This is only one tree. Numerous other trees provide different healing benefits.

Today's Druids continue to celebrate the cycles of nature and place emphasis on the importance of planting trees. Mature trees produce enough oxygen for ten people, clean the air of pollutants, provide shelter and food for animals, ease drought by soaking up gallons of water from the ground to be released from its leaves into the air, and many other benefits. While planting trees is one of the best things you can do for the earth, you cannot replace the loss of mature trees cut down for logging purposes on the Appalachian Trail by planting a sapling to replace it. When we lose mature trees, we lose the healing benefits that they provide, which will take many, many years to replace. Consider joining the Arbor Society and other organizations aimed at not only planting trees, but preserving ancient forest in danger of being cut down for our

selfish ends. This is another way to connect with nature. Instead of merely reaping its benefits, you will be giving back and enjoying the community of like-minded people in the process.

Many scientific studies have been conducted on the neurobiology of plants and trees. Scientists have discovered that plants produce chemical and electrical signals that mimic those of humans and animals on some levels, such as the chemicals that are similar to our neurotransmitters. Just as we respond to elements in our environment through touch, taste, sound, sight and hearing, so do plants, in their own way. Plants have been known to wrap themselves around pipes through which water flowed, even if there was no water on the outside of the pipe. This has led some ecologists to believe that the plant could "hear" the water going through the pipe. They also recognize their own kin and engage in both competitive and cooperative "behaviors."

Plants and trees also communicate with each other by releasing chemicals. Oak trees naturally produce a toxin that wards off invaders, for example, and if one oak is being attacked by an invader, it sends out chemical signals to the surrounding oaks. Knowing that the invader is on its way, these oaks increase their levels of this toxin. Although plants and trees don't have neurons and a nervous system the way we do, this controversial scientific research into plant "intelligence" does suggest the possibility that intelligence, learning and behavior may not require a nervous system. Perhaps the Native Americans, Druids and other similar traditions are correct in stating that everything in nature has spirit and consciousness. Considering that plants and trees make up much more of the earth than we do, we should give

them more respect. If we are all part of one consciousness, then what we do unto others, whether the others are plants, animals or people, we do unto ourselves.

Make friends with your local forest and the trees in your neighborhood. Hike in an ancient forest, or visit a forest with the oldest trees you can find. Find a comfortable rock, and breathe deeply and slowly for several minutes. As you breathe, know that you are breathing in the breath of trees. The trees, in turn, are breathing in your breath as you exhale. You are becoming one with the trees and experiencing an intimate connection you may have been taking for granted. Continue doing this until the boundaries between you and the trees dissolve into oneness.

Celebrate

Create your own rituals to celebrate the change of seasons or explore nature-based spirituality, such as Druidry, to learn some rituals and to connect with nature on a deeper level. Performing rituals to celebrate and honor the change of seasons, which also reflect our fluctuating mental states and the seasons of our own lives, is both grounding and inspiring. Life is a cycle, not a beginning and ending. Forms pop into and out of existence, but the essence never dies.

The modern Druids have eight beautiful, seasonal celebrations. You can try them yourself or create your own, based on your religion or spiritual path of choice. Samhuinn, for example, is the beginning of the Celtic year and means "summer's end." Celebrated on or around the first of November, Druids honor the cycle of life, which is an endless wheel of beginnings and endings. At Samhuinn, the veil that separates our world from the otherworld is thin, allowing us

closer contact with those who have passed on before us. Rather than death being an ending, the Druids view it as entering another doorway. Thus, Samhuinn is also a way to honor the dead. The arrival of the Christians did not change this tradition. Instead, they created their own holy day to honor the dead that also occurs at this time: All Souls' Day.

Whether you are Christian, Hindu, Jewish, Muslim, Atheist or follow some other spiritual path, you can still celebrate the cycles of nature. Today's Druids decorate an altar with various items from nature, depending on the season. For Samhuinn, for example, they might go to the woods to gather some colorful fall leaves to add to the altar. Four bowls are set in each of the four corners, representing the elements of earth (clean dirt or salt), air (incense), fire (votive candle) and water (purified water). These bowls also correspond to the four directions. The celebration includes several ritualistic aspects, as well as a beautiful meditation on this particular season. I won't go into further detail here, but I have listed a reference in the Works Cited section that contains details on how to perform the Druid ceremonies.

To honor the changes of the seasons and to cleanse my body in preparation for the new season and the new foods that come with it, I engage in a day of fasting and meditation. That day, I may sip on herbal teas, vegetable broth, homemade vegetable juice and warm lemon water. I also take cleansing herbs to clean out the toxins that may have built up that season. Fasting allows the body to take a break from digestion and your mind to take a break from meal planning. Instead, you devote your time to spiritual development. You can gain powerful insight as a result of the space you have created.

My friend and fellow health coach, Sarah, loves ritual. To

celebrate the change in seasons, she might wear a brightly-colored shirt that represents the new season, create space for the season by cleaning out her closets, or invite her friends over for a potluck consisting of seasonal foods. Celebrating the seasons is a powerful way to connect ourselves to nature and to be grateful for the present moment. We are often so caught up in the snares of our hectic, complicated lives that the seasons pass us by without much notice. Find a way to take time to reflect on the season that is passing, and welcome the new season, whether you use an existing ritual or create a tradition of your own.

Spend time with animals.

While visiting my parents, I once walked out to the barn, sat on the fence, and played my Native American cedar flute. As if mesmerized, my parents' horses slowly came in from the pasture and up to the fence. Gradually, I found myself surrounded by these wide-eyed, gentle animals while I played. When I told my dad about it, he showed no trace of surprise and simply responded that animals like music, as if it were common knowledge. So play your piano for the cat or jam on your guitar for the dog. Hug your pet, or if you don't have one, hug someone else's. They will love you, even if you have morning breath or a bad haircut or have been out of work for three months. Offer to walk a neighbor's dog or cat-sit for free. Volunteer at an animal shelter. Watch the squirrels play on your lawn.

I became more interested in birds after we set out a humming bird feeder. Humming birds are such beautiful, tender creatures. I'm delighted and surprised every time I hear the magical sound of their little wings as they hover at the feeder. Try joining the Audubon Society or take a bird-watching class

to learn how to recognize birds by their calls. Learn the sounds of other animals and then see if you can recognize them while on a walk in the woods. What sound does the fox *really* make? What about a coyote? A hawk? A deer? (Yes, deer make sounds!) Learn to recognize the footsteps of various animals. What does a dog sound like as it walks through the woods versus a deer, squirrel or human?

Ecopsychology: Where Mind and Nature Meet

Ecopsychology, also referred to as ecotherapy and earth-centered therapy, is the study of the relationship between humans and the natural world through psychology and ecology. Seeking to foster a positive relationship between the two, this new science is proving the benefits of increased time in nature. Can you include more nature in your home or office? In addition to having potted herbs or a tower garden to grow food, you could buy an indoor tree and some plants. They help detoxify the air, which is particularly important in winter, when we tend to have the windows closed, forcing us to breathe in stale, heated air rather than the fresh air of the natural world. NASA did a study to find out which plants were the best at filtering the air at the space station. Among the top fifteen were English ivy, pot mum, peace lily and bamboo palm. These plants were not only adept at producing oxygen from CO2, but were also able to filter out toxic chemicals.

Thus, in addition to going out into nature, you can bring some nature into your home, thereby creating a blurred, rather than distinct, boundary between ourselves and the natural world. In reality, we are also part of the natural world, but we have taken ourselves out of it through modernization. When we go back to our roots, even in small steps, we can experience

significant stress relief by realizing we are part of the natural world and not separate from it. When this occurs, we will be more inclined to take care of our planet and work with it, rather than against it.

Chapter 1 ~ Walk the Path

1. Take time to study the ecology of the area in which you live. State and national parks are good resources, as well as your local library or used bookstore. Join your local Audubon Society and Arbor Society.
2. Look around you at the leaves on the tree or ground. How many leaf varieties do you see? What about the flowers and plants around you? Do you recognize them all? If not, start learning about your local trees and plant life, and then see if you can recognize more and more plants and trees the next time you explore.
3. Sit for twenty minutes and write down how many sounds you hear. At first, you may only hear a bird and the wind blowing through the trees. Keep listening. You will notice more and more sounds. Eventually, you may notice the sound of insects crawling across the leaves, a squirrel jumping from one tree limb to another, and additional bird calls. Perhaps you will be inspired to take a bird-watching class and learn to name birds by their calls.
4. For a week, challenge yourself to be in nature daily, perhaps in a local park, your own garden, or a small wooded area near your work place. Walk slowly, inhale deeply, and notice the variety of plant and animal life that surrounds you. You can even do this in winter by standing in a sheltered area and noticing what wildlife decided to brave the cold. I was surprised at the number of birds that decided to stick it out over the winter. Fresh air is something we don't get enough of during the winter months, so even a few minutes in nature per day can make a huge difference. How do you feel at the end of the week?

5. Try a tree breathing meditation: http://www.druidry.org/druid-way/teaching-and-practice/druidry-meditation/deep-peace-tree-meditation

Chapter 2

The Monk's Path ~ The Art of Reflection and Stillness

"The space between your thoughts is the window to the cosmic mind" ~ Deepak Chopra

When we are born, the first thing we do is inhale. When we die or cross over, the last thing we do on this earth is exhale. Breath is the link between body and spirit, and how we breathe affects our emotions as well as our thoughts. It is also an important component of yoga and meditation. If prayer is talking to God, the Great Spirit, Buddha or whomever, then meditation is when you listen. We spend so much time talking, whether gossiping with others or engaging in ceaseless mental chatter, that we fail to take the time to go inward and truly listen. If we can calm our over-active minds, then we can gain insight that transcends pure logic or reason. Monks of various spiritual traditions spend a large portion of their day meditating, allowing them to create a calm mind that is open to amazing insight and revelation.

Marty Wuttke is a well-known neuro-biofeedback specialist who has studied the effects of meditation on the brain. I was fortunate enough to attend a lecture he gave at the Center for Spiritual Enlightenment in San Jose, CA. "The human nervous system is the vehicle for God," he explained during the lecture. The good news is that we have more control over our nervous system than we might think. Wuttke hooked up various monks to an EEG that allowed him to observe the monks' ability to control their brain waves and various bodily functions at will. There was a significant difference between the brains of these monks, who meditated regularly, and non-

meditators. The monks were able to control their brain activity, including increasing various types of brain waves, such as Theta, at will. They could also control physiological aspects of their bodies, such as temperature and heart rate. Meditation is not just for monks, though. For example, research has shown the benefits of meditation on people with depression, anxiety and ADHD, or who are suffering from addiction and trauma.

To meditate effectively, focusing on the breath is a great start. For the next week, simply observe your breath while doing various activities. Do you notice yourself breathing shallowly when you are stressed, or even holding your breath while doing certain activities? When we are tense, we often breathe shallowly from the upper register of our chest with our shoulders up to our ears. This creates even more tension. When I started really paying attention to my breathing, I noticed I was often holding my breath without realizing it, especially when I was doing something that required concentration. Think about it. When you are reading a stressful email at work, putting on your mascara in the morning or shaving, check your breathing. I'll bet it's not deep and regular, but rather shallow and higher up in the chest. In fact, you may go several seconds without breathing at all, just like I was doing. This creates a stress response in the body, exacerbating the situation.

If you are a Type A like me, setting a reminder on your phone to check your breathing once an hour might appeal to you. If you'd rather not use technology, focus on checking your breath and your posture each time you switch to a new activity. Notice how breathing deeply creates relaxation in the body and mind. Make it a habit to do this regularly. I

incorporate breath work into my yoga and meditation practice, but also my daily activities, including doing the laundry, shaving my legs, ice skating or writing this book. When I do so, I am more focused, more relaxed and more clear-headed. One of the reasons I find swimming so relaxing is that my breathing is slow, deep and rhythmic. What ways can you coordinate your breath with your movement when you vacuum, rake the leaves or engage in your favorite sport?

I learned in yoga class that abdominal breathing stimulates the vagas nerve, which helps you manage stress and improve digestion. Relax your shoulders and breathe deeply and slowly. Place your hand on your abdomen. It should be moving in and out. Continue to do this while visualizing the breath going in and out of the center of your chest or heart. Breathe in for several seconds, hold your breath for a moment, and then breathe out several seconds. Your breathing should be slow, even and smooth. Even if you only do this one exercise, you will benefit enormously. As a health coach, the HeartMath® program is one of the many tools I use to help my clients tap into their heart wisdom. The heart contains over 40,000 neurons! Scientists at the Institute of HeartMath® have figured out ways to tap into this highly-intuitive wisdom. Although this has to be taught by a coach rather than a book, the above exercise is a good one to get you started, since proper breathing is the foundation of many wellness programs.

For more advanced work with breath, try various "pranayamas," or breathing techniques, to increase what Indians call "prana" or what the Chinese call "chi." Loosely translated, prana means "life force." BKS Iyengar, who is known for popularizing yoga worldwide, defines pranayama

as the "...conscious prolongation of inhalation, retention and exhalation." I've listed a few at the end of this chapter, but you can learn many more through organizations such as the Art of Living Foundation or a yoga studio. These breathing practices are great ways to start and end your day. Try them in the middle of the day to ease tension, increase energy and bring yourself back to the present moment. I often do these practices before, during and/or after a stressful event. Practice breath work and meditation when you are both calm and stressed, though, since regular practice will help you develop the skills and automaticity needed to use them in high-stress situations. Consider them part of your daily medicine.

Sitting Meditation

There are many ways to practice sitting meditation. If you are new to meditation or feel you just cannot meditate, try what I call "cloud watching." Just sit quietly for about five minutes and watch for "clouds" or thoughts. Your job is not to judge these thoughts as good or bad, but to assign a non-emotional label, such as "future thinking," "planning," "memory," etc. Even if you visualize killing your boss, you do not judge this by telling yourself it is wrong to think this way or that you must be crazy. You simply assign a label (problem-solving -- ha!) and allow the thought to drift away until the next one drifts into view. Easy, right? This is a form of meditation!

A great way to practice meditation is by doing it in a group. I first learned meditation at the Shambhala Centre in London. There are Shambhala centers all around the world, and they are great at helping beginning meditators. I was taught on a one-to-one basis and could ask questions about the process before joining the group. Organizations such as The Art of Living Foundation teach a variety of classes that are not

limited to meditation. For example, the organization offers a silent meditation retreat, yoga classes, Ayurvedic cooking classes, and much more. Many Buddhist monasteries have classes available to the public, or you can join a sangha or group, which usually offers group meditation and "dharma talks." Other religious traditions also have meditative practices. Catholics, for example, pray the rosary, which is a form of meditation. Do what works for you.

Discursive Meditation

Unlike the "empty mind" meditation of the east, during discursive meditation, the meditator focuses her mind on a thought, image, concept, short exerpt from a spiritual text, etc. Pursuing these trains of thought and observing how they evolve is at the crux of discursive meditation. If you are trying to understand a spiritual text or solve a problem, you could ponder the question in an evening meditation or reflection, sleep on it, and then ask your question early the next morning as you engage in discursive meditation. This might keep someone like me awake, though, so as an alternative, you could simply wait until morning to ponder the question. Engaging in any kind of meditation first thing in the morning allows you to take advantage of your mind's censor not being fully awake. If you find your mind wandering, trace your most recent thought to its origin.

Active and Mindful Meditation

You can incorporate meditative practices into everyday activities, just like breath. Sitting for ten to twenty minutes each morning and/or evening is a great start, but incorporating the practice into everyday life gives it much more power, just as praying one day a week at church, mosque or temple is not

as powerful as walking a spiritual path daily in all activities. Make doing the dishes or mowing the yard a meditation. What smells, sounds and other sensations do you notice? See if you can put all of your focus on the task you are performing, whether it's brushing your teeth or walking the dog. Do you notice any details that you may have missed because you were always thinking about something else?

Marion Frick-Rigsbee, a friend of mine who is a therapist here in Indianapolis, has a great mindfulness technique. Every day, she spends a few minutes going through each of her senses and noting any sensations. This is something anyone can do any time. For example, if you're sitting in a coffee shop, take in the visual details of your surroundings, such as the wooden ceilings, matching hardwood floors, and the stone hearth, which give the shop a cabin-like feel. When examining taste, even if you are not eating, perhaps you will still notice different tastes in your mouth, such as the aftertaste of coffee and the cream you added to it. When you move on to smell, what layers of smell exist at the moment? You may only smell coffee at first. But upon further probing, perhaps you can detect your own perfume, the sweet, buttery smell of pastry the person next to you is eating, or the lemon cleaner used on the floors earlier that morning. Notice the hardness of the chair on which you are sitting, the floor beneath your feet, and the way the clothes feel on your body, such as the softness of the merino wool socks you are wearing. Also note any internal sensations you feel, such as a gargling stomach that is ready for more than coffee.

The Art of Letting Go

I've studied spiritual practices of many traditions, and one of the primary lessons I've learned from Buddhism is how to let

go. Meditation and other practices teach practitioners how to let go of judgment, of "forcing" an outcome, and of attachments. THIS IS SO HARD! Many of us are so driven and are so adept at persevering that it's hard not to *force* something to happen. One of my meditation teachers is also a very intense, driven person. During a "dokasan" or one-on-one, we talked about how to let go without being passive. He instructed me to put out the intention, take action, and then let go to some degree. When we do this, the universe will guide us.

When you really want something, where do you feel it in your body? Many times, we feel it in the middle of our torso, or solar plexus region, which is associated with our "will." When Christians pray, they say "Thy will be done" as part of a prayer, but how many of us actually let go enough for the divine will, universe, or whatever you want to call it, to guide us? Can you think of a time you were in "flow"? Everything just fell into place without much effort. Now think of a time when you chased after something and expended tons of energy to reach your goal, only to realize a better path had been available all along. This happened to me many times in the past. I shudder to think of how many days, weeks and even years of energy I've lost unnecessarily. Sometimes what we want isn't what's truly best. Setting intentions and then letting go allows our intuition and the universe to be our guide.

I put this into practice when my husband and I were deciding whether or not to move from the Bay Area, California to Portland, Oregon. We visited Portland a few times and LOVED it. I put my intentions out there by putting in effort, such as applying for jobs and networking. Then, I let go of my

attachment to the outcome. Although I met many nice, helpful people, things were not in flow. Nothing happened. So we looked at another alternative: Indianapolis. All of my family lives in Indiana, housing is even more affordable here than in Portland, and there are four distinct seasons, which I love. When we started putting feelers out there, everything just came together, as if the stars aligned just for me to make it happen. For example, I met a man on the plane ride to Indianapolis who was the CEO of a classical music station. He helped me get connected in the area and then asked me to be a regular writer for the station's magazine. The whole process of buying a house was easy. There wasn't a single hitch, and closing was stress-free. A week after closing, my mortgage broker invited me to a networking group that yielded two clients within the first six weeks. The key is to have compassion for yourself, rather than trying to force something to happen or becoming angry when you can't see the solution right away.

As you grow on your spiritual path, you will most certainly encounter obstacles. This seems to happen more strongly during meditation, when you are trying to still the mind. You may feel an itch on your leg, and then your knee might start to hurt, causing you to change positions. The next thing you know, you can't sit still. Or perhaps a disturbing thought will enter your mind, causing you to think you must be possessed by a demon to think such a thing. Or you might find that you can only sit for a couple of seconds before your mind drifts off with its list-making, problem-solving or fantasy-engaging. You will be tempted to give up, because trying to find that deep, silent well within is frustrating, stressful and even frightening. Keep walking the path. These thoughts, feelings and sensations are a result of your ego trying to reassert itself.

Your ego is like a two-year-old child who depends on your attention, and when you turn from ego to soul, the ego's existence might feel threatened. It will throw a fit. It feels that you are going to abandon it and that it will die.

Sri Sri Ravi Shankar, who people in the Art of Living call "Guruji," said "Every moment you should die. Then you can be alive. Every moment there is death." Allowing yourself to change is death. Dropping thoughts, feelings and habits that no longer serve you is death. Ending an abusive relationship is death. Death is sometimes necessary to allow you to live. However, we don't want ego to die. Like everything else, it has its purpose. One of my fellow meditators said she pretends her ego is like a big polar bear. When she sits down to meditate, she sends the bear off with a big beach ball to play with for the next hour until she is finished. I sometimes talk to my ego as if I were trying to calm an upset child; I let it know I'll be back soon, that it is safe, and that everything will be okay. Then I sit, I breathe, and I let go.

Chapter 2 ~ Walk the Path

1. *Alternate nostril breathing*: Cover your right nostril with your right thumb. Rest your index and middle fingers in between your eyebrows or "third eye." Breathe in through your left nostril for seven seconds. Hold for two seconds as you uncover your right nostril and use your ring finger to cover your left nostril. Breathe out for seven seconds through your right nostril and then hold for two seconds. Breathe in through your right nostril for seven seconds, hold for two seconds as you cover your right nostril with your thumb again and uncover your left nostril. Breathe out for seven seconds through your left nostril. Begin the process again by breathing in through the left nostril for seven seconds, hold for two seconds as you cover your left nostril and uncover your right nostril. Breathe out for seven seconds, etc. There are different ways to perform this technique, but this is what works for me. Don't get too hung up on the number of seconds. This activity is great for balancing both sides of the brain, creating equilibrium. I recommend doing this throughout the day to continually bring balance.
2. *Tonglen*: This is a Buddhist practice, but it can be used regardless of religious beliefs. When you are really wound up and find yourself in a ceaseless whirlpool of negative thinking, imagine you are inhaling all the black, sticky, negative goo of your thoughts. Instead of repressing it, you are accepting it. When you exhale, visualize you are exhaling pure, white light. This is a spiritual alchemy of sorts, because you are transforming the negative into the positive or "gold." Many people try to repress the negative in various ways, but this allows you to face it head on and transform it. Keep performing this until the negative whirlpool ceases. This is a powerful practice and can be done anywhere at any time.

3. *Ujjayi breath*: This is a must for anyone wanting to attend a yoga class and should be combined with the abdominal breathing mentioned earlier. Due to its heating quality, teachers routinely remind students to use their ujjayi breath or "victorious" breath while performing various asanas. Even if you don't plan to do yoga, you can use this breath when you are feeling angry or frustrated. Take a deep inhale and constrict your throat muscles. Do the same when you exhale. It should make a sound reminiscent of the ocean. Sarah Diedrick, a yoga teacher in Vermont, uses the imagery of a wave as she performs this pranayama. She imagines her belly is a wave coming in from ocean and back out.
4. Keep a twenty-one day meditation journal. Notice any patterns or changes that arise.
5. Light a candle in the dark and gaze into the flame. Notice how it dances in response to an imperceptible current of air, and then holds steady for a period of time. Watch it grow and then diminish. What can you learn from your observations?
6. Use prayer beads to meditate on a theme.
7. Meditate on an image of a guru, saint or deity who speaks to you.
8. Start out meditating five minutes at a time, and gradually work your way up to twenty, thirty, forty minutes.
9. Attend a formal meditation class.
10. Listen to a guided meditation on a CD.

Chapter 3

The Artist's Path ~ Unlock Your Creative Flow

"You can't use up creativity. The more you use, the more you have." ~ Maya Angelou

The poets of the English Romantic period were on a constant quest for for the transcendental, sublime experience, and revered the wildness of the natural world due to its ability to bring about such an experience. Perhaps the craggy, granite mountains of the Alps, with their treacherous narrow pathways that sometimes led to the traveler to his death, were the epitome of the sublime in nature. The sheer size of Mont Blanc, the highest point in the Alps, was a reminder of man's insignificance compared to the forces of nature. When beholding such a giant, one is overpowered, as if in the presence of a god. William Wordsworth was one of many who crossed the Alps during this time period. In his epic poem, *The Prelude,* he describes the sublime experience of crossing the Alps as "the light of sense" having been "snuffed out." The overpowering of the senses led to an illumination of the inner world of the mind and the imagination.

Regular time in nature, as mentioned in the first chapter, has many benefits. Not only does it relax the mind, but it inspires creativity. Many moments of inspiration came to me from time spent in nature, such as watching the sun disappear into the turquoise ocean of Key West, lighting the sky in vermillion and orange, or stepping outside in the middle of winter to experience the quiet solitude that occurs when the world is covered in a blanket of snow. Memories such as these can rise up unexpectedly in the form of inspiration. Becoming fused

with the imagination, they may evolve into paintings, sculptures, or poetry.

Rather than waiting for moments of inspiration to arise, engage in a creative activity daily. Even if most of what you produce is rubbish in your opinion, it's important to do the work regularly. Many successful artists will tell you that it is by performing the work regularly that you invite inspiration. If you wait until you are inspired to pursue your artistic endeavors, you will create very little. Most days that I sit down to write, I am not inspired. During a lecture I attended, JM Coetzee gave the following advice for a writing routine: "You sit down in front of a blank computer screen or piece of paper and hope for the best. And you do it every day." Inspiration often hits after I've been writing for several minutes. Sometimes, it doesn't happen at all. The important thing is that I do it daily, and this daily act of creativity is what enables me to lead an inspired life. Whether you consider yourself an artist or not, everyone has the ability to create. Creating allows us to participate with the Great Creator; therefore, it's a divine act that puts us in touch with our own divinity, which often gets lost in the lists of errands and piles of bills to be paid.

Journal Daily

In her book *The Artist's Way*, Julia Cameron recommends journaling as a great way to detox your mind to allow room for creativity to enter. She recommends doing it first thing in the morning, but in order to reflect on the day and empty the mental trash, some find it helpful to do it at night after dinner when things have slowed down. Do what works for you. Journaling regularly is a must for most writers, but it can lead to creativity in other endeavors as well. One of my clients, an

aspiring artist, couldn't find the time for her art, exercise and self-care in general as a result of being exhausted by both motherhood and business concerns. I suggested *The Artist's Way*. She bought it and started doing the lessons within the book, particularly the morning pages. As she did so, repressed negative thoughts started to find their way to the surface, enabling her to deal with them directly. Through this exercise in working through creative blockage, my client had an epiphany about two areas of her life that weren't directly related to her artistic work, but that certainly impacted it. She realizes that her art is like "breathing" to her, and so now that she sees it as a necessity rather than a selfish endeavor, she is able to make more time for exercise and other areas she had been neglecting. Meditation works the same way. If you take the time to do it, you end up having more time in your day.

While journaling, I note any frustrations or negative feelings that come to the surface, creating room for more creative, inspiring thoughts. Try free writing for at least ten minutes without censoring yourself. If you can't think of what to write, just keep writing "I don't know what to write" until something else pops up. Keep your hand moving. Journaling can be another form of meditation in the sense that we are paying attention to our thoughts rather than walking around only half conscious of them. When these negative thoughts arise, I search for the root. Where is this coming from? Since I'm already in a meditative state, I'm in the right frame of mind to categorize these thoughts. It all boils down to ego and to letting go. Being aware of the thoughts, I am able to neutralize these negative feelings by coming up with a positive alternative. I also do Tonglen at this point (see chapter 2), inhaling the black, oozy, stickiness of negativity and exhaling pure white light. There's always more than one

way to look at something. Unfortunately, many of us choose the negative interpretation. This practice of journaling can be crucial to working on mitigating these negative feelings before you have the chance to perpetuate the problem further through speech or action. A creative way of mitigating the negative thoughts about a person is through empathy. Artists are great empathizers. They walk the path of others in order to feel what they feel, then express this to the world through a character in a book or the subject of a sculpture.

During the twelve-week self-study course outlined in *The Artist's Way*, Cameron suggests many other exercises to allow your creativity to unfold. When I followed the course, it felt like a pleasant "trip" without all of the negative side effects. Colors started popping out more vividly, and I explored working with mosaics and painting with pastels. I was never a great art student, so I was shocked by the things I created.

Reading is a great way to find inspiration for writing, whether you are journaling, writing non-fiction or working on a novel. I start the creative process by reading poetry or a short passage from an inspirational book. Good writers are usually avid readers, and even if you aren't an aspiring writer, reading and journaling can help you clear your mind, shift your perspective, and allow the creative process to unfold.

Pick a hobby

Pick up an old hobby AND start a new one. Think you are a horrible painter and can only draw stick people? Take a painting class anyway. I got a D in sewing in 8th grade, which was the class that kept me off the honor roll, but I joined a knitting group as an adult. I not only learned to knit, but made friends in the process. Learn how to can food or bake

gluten-free bread, even if you are not known for your culinary talents. As Eleanor Roosevelt said, "Do the things you think you cannot do." It's so empowering! After I did my first jump as an ice skater, I was able to deal with a difficult client later that morning with 100% confidence and calm. I never skated once as a child, so learning to skate in my late thirties was a bit daunting, but I have stuck with it. I am inspired by people in their fifties still doing jumps and spins, and with much more finesse than I have. Recently, I performed in my first ice skating show with a group of adult skaters. It was one of the scariest things I've ever done, but I'm much more courageous in everyday life as a result.

Engaging in a hobby is a great way to meet other people, but it also keeps you mentally challenged, which is important as we age. My grandmother learned to paint when she was seventy and discovered she was a talented painter. My grandfather learned to use a computer in his seventies and made it a hobby to find interesting facts online. A former ESL student of mine practiced yoga daily, which included standing on his head. He was ninety! My husband's ninety-four year-old grandfather swam daily in the spring-fed river behind his house until recently. No, he didn't die. The river dried up. Now, he spends most of his day reading and listening to classes on CDs that he receives through the *Great Courses*. Do you see a trend here? It's never too late, so no excuses!!!

Make Music

Pick your guitar back up or learn to play an instrument if you've never learned to play one. The Native American cedar flute is easy to learn to play: there are no notes to read, and the sound is soothing and beautiful. Invite some friends over and ask everyone to bring an instrument, even if it's a tambourine

or other simple instrument. One of my friends did this once. I brought my cedar flute, and one of her friends brought a saxophone. He "followed" me on the sax as I played my flute, and the others in the group provided background music with tambourines and a small drum. Who knew that all of these instruments could sound good together? It was such a creative release. I felt as if I'd had a mental message combined with a cup of coffee. If you and your friends aren't musical, you can bang pots and pans. Who cares? It's fun!

You can even join a drum circle, which doesn't require musical expertise. I joined one recently and can't believe I didn't do it earlier in life. I brought my little hand drum that I had never really played. One of the facilitators of the circle showed us some of the basics. The drummer responsible for the "base" beat, or the heartbeat of the circle, started us off. Each of us joined in when we could feel a calling towards a particular rhythm. The result was pure magic. I entered into a meditative, trance-like state as I felt one with the pulse of the group. The drum beats spoke to something primal and ancient in me, and I allowed myself to be carried away on the tide. We were each playing a beat that called to us as individuals, but remained in harmony with the rest of the group. This was a great lesson for how to live life.

If you don't have a musical instrument and can't afford one right now, sing. Even if you aren't a talented singer, nature gave you your own instrument. Try singing in the shower. The acoustics will make nearly everyone's voice sound decent. My grandmother was tone deaf, and much to my dismay, she sang as loudly as she could at mass on Sundays, causing children to giggle. As she used to say, "God gave me this voice, so he's gonna have to listen to it." If you discover that

you enjoy singing, try joining the local choir. It will connect you with others while providing an excellent outlet for stress. It will also increase your musical talent, since you will have scheduled, regular practice times. If you celebrate Christmas, you could even join a madrigal choir during the holiday season. My mom used to sing in one, and I remember how enriched the holiday season felt as a result.

Explore different music styles to discover the type of music that inspires you and relaxes you. Which songs elicit the most powerful memories? Note your emotional responses to certain pieces. For example, when I hear Vivaldi's Flautino Concerto in E minor, my mind feels free and expansive. When I listen to Jacqueline du Pre play Elgar's Cello Concerto in E minor, my chest feels tight with emotion, as if the emotions of both composer and musician are flowing into me at once in a powerful rush. I even get goose bumps on my arm. While I love this piece, this is not the music I listen to if I want to relax and feel at peace. Instead, I might listen to Joshua Bell playing one of Chopin's nocturnes or Carlos Nakai playing the Native American cedar flute.

Go to a concert to hear your favorite band, listen to a local band in a coffee shop, or go to a symphony performance. Hearing live music affects you in a way that listening to the radio or a CD doesn't. It vibrates through you, and the air is charged with the energy of the others in the concert hall. Listening to music live can release toxic emotions, provided that you are at the right kind of concert! It can also ignite the creative process, whether you are playing an instrument or just listening to one. You are able to draw from the energy of others and bond with those around you. Live music also allows you to have the combined benefit of the structure

within the musical score and the spontaneity of your emotional and physical response.

Play like a child

As adults, we forget how to let go and have fun. Children are great teachers when it comes to play. Observe them. They scream, jump up and down, get dirty, explore new things, find entertainment in the ordinary and make a mess. Try finger painting, swinging on a swing set, climbing a tree or digging a hole in the sand. Walk across fallen logs. Build a snowman. Bang on a bongo drum and make as much noise as possible. Sing at the top of your lungs. Slide across the tile in your socks. Find as many uses for a stick as possible: sword? baton? javelin? magic wand? Make a house out of popsicle sticks and other items from around the house. Explore, play and focus on the moment. If it helps, do this with a child. Let her lead.

Be Spontaneous

While there is a definite benefit to being a highly-structured person, even in the creative process, spontaneity is also important. In *The Artist's Way*, Julia Cameron encourages her aspiring artists to go on an "artist date" every week. This "date"must be done alone. When I did the course, I went on long hikes, took trips to art museums and antique shops, and covered a wooden tray in a mosaic design. Engage in a spontaneous activity this week. Walk into an herb shop, go Meade tasting, or do a drop-in pottery or dance class. If you need a bit more planning to feel comfortable, look at community alternative newspapers and pick out an event to attend. When you are there, go with your impulse. Try something that makes you a tiny bit uncomfortable, allowing

yourself to let go in order to expand.

Chapter 3 ~ Walk the Path

1. Do something creative every day this week, even if you have to get up ten minutes earlier.
2. Make up a dance routine to your favorite song.
3. Finger paint with your kids, nieces, nephews or neighbor's kid.
4. Try an interesting new recipe.
6. Hire an art therapist.
7. Do something that scares you.
8. Create a collage of your favorite things.

Chapter 4

The Shamanic Path ~ The Healing Magic of Food

"Let food be thy medicine and medicine by thy food" – Hippocrates

In *The Way of Wyrd,* a Celtic shaman agrees to allow a Christian scribe to be his apprentice. The scribe's job was to record the religion of the pagans in Britain so this knowledge could be used to convert them to Christianity. The shaman, named Wulf, was unafraid of the strange noises in the dark of the forest. In fact, he was quite at home in the wilderness, where he hunted for magical herbs that he would use, along with various chants, to heal the sick. Wulf's practices seemed primitive and barbaric to his apprentice at first, but when he witnessed time and time again the efficacy of Wulf's practices, he questioned his own belief system.

Herbs and other foods have been used for thousands of years to heal others physically, emotionally and spiritually. Unfortunately, there is much more money in researching and developing pharmaceutical drugs, and so herbs and healing foods do not get nearly the scientific attention they deserve. As a result, people are taking drugs with horrible side effects, when healing through natural medicine, such as herbs and dietary and lifestyle changes might have helped the person heal in a way that worked with their body's chemistry and natural healing processes. According to *Consumer Report Magazine,* 80,000 people were sent to the ER last year from liver toxicity due to taking acetaminophen. People are returning to the old ways for healing, trusting in the thousands of years of anecdotal evidence of their effectiveness, because our current system of healing in the Western world is

broken.

I am a good example of this. From the time I was very young, I experienced issues with my blood sugar. No matter how much I ate, I would be "starving" a few hours later. My parents would tell me to eat more so I wouldn't be hungry so often, but I was eating as much as I could. Some people thought I just had a high metabolism because I was an active kid and naturally thin. My mom suspected I had diabetes and took me to get my blood sugar tested on a few occasions. The doctors always had the same response: I didn't have diabetes. What I realized later was that, although my symptoms couldn't be fit neatly enough into a box to get a diagnosis, I knew one thing for sure: my body had a hard time controlling blood sugar.

While labels can be helpful, they can sometimes encourage black and white thinking. Part of the reason I enrolled in nutrition school was to heal myself of the blood sugar spikes and crashes that resulted in extreme irritability, tunnel vision, nausea and mood swings. At the time I enrolled at the Institute of Integrative Nutrition, I was working with many people who had ADHD. I noticed that when they consumed sugar, refined carbs, and foods with artificial flavors and colors, their ability to focus was greatly impaired. These experiences in my personal and professional life led me on the path of nutrition.

Pharmaceutical drugs are sometimes necessary, and I am forever grateful to the scientists working on finding a cure for Ebola, for example. But in my opinion, drugs are greatly overprescribed, especially for chronic conditions. Food is nature's medicine. Eating real, whole foods can bring healing to the body and mind, while "fake" foods that inundate our

supermarkets and restaurants today can wreak havoc on our health. Nutrition is fascinating due to its huge impact on our emotions, energy level, ability to sleep, stress levels, hormones, and everything else about our lives. The food you eat talks to your DNA and either turns genes on or off, depending on the messages you send. You may have a genetic predisposition to depression, but your lifestyle and the foods you eat have a great deal to do with whether or not those genes are activated. The science of epigenetics is proving this to be the case. I know this because I have experienced it directly. Through eating foods that resonated with my bio-individuality, using nature's medicine to heal, and making lifestyle changes, such as having a strong spiritual path that included meditation, I was able to cure myself of the blood sugar peaks and valleys and the dark moods that had plagued me my entire life.

It's not only what you eat, but the environment in which you prepare and consume food and how and where the food was grown, that contribute to food's healing effects. This chapter will draw upon methods for using food physically, mentally and spiritually in order to heal ourselves on all of these levels.

Live off the land and in harmony with nature

Imagine walking out to your garden at sunrise on a summer morning, the dew still on the grass, and picking fresh berries to put on top of your oatmeal, mint to put in your cup of tea, or lettuce for a lunch-time salad. As you inhale the smell of fresh dirt and honeysuckle, you hear the sounds of at least five different birds heralding a new day as a startled chipmunk darts up a nearby tree. This garden benefits you, but it also supports the natural world around you. Birds drink from the birdbath full of pure rainwater, bees pollinate your flowers,

and animals of all sorts eat the fruit that falls from the apple tree. Sure, much of the fruit rots before you can eat it, but the animals and insects thrive on this fallen food. The surrounding trees appreciate it when you mulch it back into the soil, further enriching their food supply. And because you don't spray your lawn or garden with chemicals, you don't worry as much about walking around barefoot or peeling your carrots before eating them, allowing you to draw nutrients from the soil and the skin of the plant. In fact, you may not have a lawn at all. Rather than dominating nature, you live according to its laws, and in turn, it rewards you with good health inside and out.

We spend so much of our time fighting against nature with chemical sprays to have the perfect lawn, eating foods out of season that have been grown with pesticides and herbicides, and allowing others far away to grow our food. Gain back your independence by learning to grow at least some of your own food. Plant a garden, even if it's a few pots of herbs in your window sill. If you don't have land for a garden, in addition to having herbs in your kitchen, you can rent a plot on a community garden or volunteer to work on a farm or in someone else's garden. You can even buy a "tower garden" to grow your own vegetables indoors year-round, and it doesn't take up that much space. You can grow anything in the tower garden that grows above the ground. There is nothing more satisfying than having food on the table that you grew and/or picked yourself, and it is the freshest, healthiest food in the world!

Learn to can your own vegetables during the summer months to last you through the winter. Instead of spaghetti sauce made with tomatoes grown in Italy that were processed in

China, filled with sugar and additives, and then shipped to the US to sit on a shelf for several months, you are eating sauce made from tomatoes that grew in your back yard this past summer. As you eat your dinner on chilly winter nights, the taste brings back memories of those warm summer days in your garden.

Take a permaculture class or homesteading class to increase your knowledge of how to live off the land. Since food starts to lose its nutrition from the moment it is picked, and fruits and vegetables grown far away are picked before they are even ripe, the food you grow will be far healthier. You will also be able to avoid consuming pesticides and herbicides, which are harmful to the earth and your body. Many people in urban areas have rooftop gardens and find other creative ways to be independent. Some keep bees. Others make their own soaps, shampoos and other products from herbs they grew themselves. Whichever path you choose, spending time growing and harvesting your own fruits and vegetables will connect you with the earth and the food you put into your body, allowing you to be more grounded. Gardening is also relaxing and meditative, and the connection to the natural world outside enables us to have a deeper connection to our own nature within.

Eat with the Ethiopians: Ritual and Communion

I recently dined with my husband, sister, and brother-in-law at a local Ethiopian restaurant. I've always loved Ethiopian food for its wonderful mix of spices and sour, spongy Injara bread. The owner of the restaurant gave us a short history of Ethiopia, including the fact that Christianity in Ethiopia dates back to 100 A.D and that Ethiopians were among the first to open their doors to Muslims who were being persecuted in

Saudi Arabia. Opening doors to guests and breaking bread with them is important in their culture, he explained. Ever vigilant about the second coming of Christ, they feel that a guest who comes to their door could be the Christ who has come again in a different form.

He also shared a surprising fact: women who become a master of handling spices are revered in his society and have their choice of husband. They are also considered to be spiritual masters and can hold high office in government. They realize the importance of spices for one's health, both mental and physical. Ginger, for example, is found in many dishes, and is known by many for helping with stomach upset. There is also evidence to suggest that it might also lower blood sugar.

Ethiopians also have a spiritual view of dining, he explained. They believe that when you dine, you are not only in communion with the people with whom you are sharing food, but that angels are present. Eating is a divine act that nourishes the spirit, rather than simply a way of fueling the body. Sharing a meal is the holiest of communion, which is why people often pray before meals. In the Christian tradition, the disciples broke bread with their master and had a "last supper" together before he was killed. At the Institute of Integrative Nutrition, we learned about primary and secondary food. Primary food is not the food you eat, but rather your relationships, spirituality, and all of the other aspects that make up your life. The food on your plate is only secondary food. Meal time, therefore, is not a time to argue or discuss politics, but rather to feel grateful for the food on your plate and the others with whom you may be sharing the meal. In other words, you combine primary and secondary food during meals, creating unity of mind, body and soul, which is

an integral part of Ethiopian culture.

Mindful Eating

How many of us text or watch TV while eating or slurp down our food in an attempt to rush to get to the next item on our list? Chew your food to a pulp, and see if you can pick out all of the different tastes. Reflect on the various people and processes that came together to create this miracle on your plate: the photosynthesis that allowed the plant to grow and flourish, the soil having the right acid-alkaline balance for the plants to thrive, the farmer who cared for the animal or plant, the adequate rainfall, and all of the other small miracles that had to come together to provide nourishment for your mind and body. This plant or animal survived long enough to become food on your plate, in spite of the droughts, high winds, freezing weather, disease and other obstacles to life.

Turn eating into a ritual that that speaks to you and fits with your belief system. You could play soothing music, light a candle, eat off of colorful plates. Be sure to take your time and chew your food thoroughly, as digestion begins in the mouth. Turn the television off, put away the cell phone, and absorb the present moment. If you are with others, tune into them. Think about a positive quality in each person that you appreciate. Use this as a time to be present with one another and to truly connect.

Ayurvedic Medicine: The "Science of Life"

The Ethiopians aren't the only ones who appreciate the value of spices for one's health. Herbs and spices are used around the world, and perhaps India is a shining example of this. One of the first things you learn in Ayurveda is your primary

dosha. This is your constitution, to translate it roughly. The three doshas are vata, pitta and kapha. Although we all contain some of each dosha, most of us have a primary and secondary dosha. For example, I'm a vata-pitta. By knowing your dosha, you can understand your imbalances and what to do about them. If your "vata" is imbalanced, which is especially common in fall and winter, you will need warming foods and spices. I sense when my vata is out of balance, because I feel cold and scattered like the wind. Hot baths and grounding foods like ghee help bring me back to balance. The summer heat and high activity level tends to increase my pitta, often to the point of imbalance. In this case, I want cooling foods such as cucumber and mint, and I avoid hot, spicy foods and high-intensity exercise such as running in the heat, which causes anger to flare up, along with acne.

You can discover your dosha through the many books written about Ayurveda or by visiting an Ayurvedic practitioner, who can detect it by taking your pulse. This may sound strange if you've never been exposed to holistic healing modalities, but I make a point not to judge something one way or another until I've tested and validated it for myself. I've tried eating according to my dosha and it works! In fact, it was experimenting with Ayurveda that helped me develop an understanding of the food-mood connection and to learn how to start using food as medicine.

Another component of Ayurvedic medicine is including the six tastes – sweet, salty, sour, bitter, pungent and astringent – in each meal. This will make your meals much more satisfying, curbing cravings as a result. For example, you could make a salad with spinach (bitter), chopped red onion (pungent), pomegranates (astringent), steamed beets (sweet),

sunflower seeds (salty), and dressing made with apple cider vinegar (sour). In the west, we tend to oscillate between sweet and salty. Introducing the other flavors into your diet on a regular basis will help you become more nutritionally and emotionally balanced.

Consume non-toxic, humanely-raised food

Many animals today are factory-farmed, packed together on dense feedlots or crammed in cages, and fed foods that are unnatural for their digestive systems. This causes illness and endless suffering. Instead of enslaving people, we are enslaving animals. Whether or not you agree that animals should be eaten, there is no denying that it is our job to ensure that we respect all of life, and that if we are going to raise animals for food, we should raise and slaughter them in the most humane and healthy way possible. Finding our way back to our souls *requires* this respect.

I visited a dairy farm near my home recently and spent two hours speaking with the farmers. The cows at this farm had an acre and a half per cow, and they were happily grazing in the sunshine on an open pasture. They live to be ten years old, which is a long time for a cow to live before being slaughtered. The night before they are killed, they are transported to the location that specializes in humane slaughter. The animals are put outside to pasture to allow them time to calm down. The next morning, they are brought into the barn. The cow is calm because it thinks it is simply going in to be milked. It is killed with a special type of gun that ends its life quickly without the cow knowing what hit it. Because the cow was calm upon death, it does not have adrenaline flowing through its veins and muscles, which makes the meat much tastier, and it is a much nicer end to a cow's life versus the way this is handled

on many conventional farms.

The farmers I visited do not ever feed their cows grain, because grains upset their digestive systems, leading to disease in the cow. When cows develop these diseases as a result of their unnatural diets, antibiotics and a host of other drugs are pumped into the cow, which we end up consuming when we drink their milk. Milk has to be pasteurized to protect us from diseases that could be passed on to us from the grain-fed cows. The process of pasteurization robs the milk of vital nutrients, and so the milk we consume today is very different from the milk my father drank on the family farm years ago. Raw milk is only harmful when the cow has been grain-fed and otherwise raised unnaturally. In fact, I have consumed raw milk on a number of occasions now, and I haven't had any issues. Although it is illegal to sell raw milk in my state, you can get raw milk in health food stores in some states. In states where it is illegal to buy raw milk, you might be able to consume raw milk if you own the cow through a cow-share program.

If you are going to eat meat and consume animal products, be very careful about where you get it. Buy 100% grass-fed organic beef and organic, pasture-raised eggs. It's best to buy from local farmers and ask questions about how the animals are raised. Make sure they are raised and slaughtered humanely. A great way to do this, other than by traveling to the farm like I did, is by visiting your local farmers' market. Although these smaller farms may not be "organic," they may still practice humane raising and slaughtering of animals and raise them without antibiotics, hormones, pesticides, herbicides, etc. (Some of the smaller farms aren't certified organic because they cannot afford the high cost of

certification). Also be sure to learn about the farms that have unhealthy, inhumane practices so you can avoid them. Eat at high-quality restaurants and ask the chef where they get their meat, eggs, dairy and seafood. Many restaurants offer farm-to-table menus to support the local farms.

Humane treatment aside, animals that were raised in poor, unnatural conditions are pumped with loads of antibiotics and other drugs to extend their miserable lives. Although antibiotics and other pharmaceutical medications are sometimes necessary for both humans and animals, they are overused and wreak havoc on the digestive system. In addition to killing the bad bacteria, antibiotics destroy the beneficial intestinal flora that help us digest our food. Poor digestion can lead to intestinal permeability, bloating, constipation, food allergies and sensitivities, and many other issues. As Hippocrates said, "All disease begins in the gut." Consuming products from animals that were healthy because they were humanely raised means better health for you. And it is also the right thing to do. Your body, mind and the animals will thank you.

Do an experiment

Try dehydrating kale with some olive oil and sea salt to make yummy kale chips, get a Vitamix or other powerful blender, go raw for a week, go vegan for a week, or do Paleo (with responsibly-raised meat) for a week. By exploring new foods and observing their effects on your mind and body, you will open yourself up to new, fun and creative possibilities that may help you meet a nutritional deficiency you didn't even know you had. Some people find that by giving up certain foods, such as gluten or dairy, not only clears up physical ailments, but also mental ones. For example, many people

who give up gluten experience increased energy and a clearing of the "mental fog" that has plagued them for so long. One of my friends said she realized she had a gluten intolerance when she connected her unusual crying episodes and low moods with gluten consumption.

Open nature's medicine cabinet

There are many herbs, teas and tinctures aimed at helping you relax, such as valerian, lemon balm, and camomile. I use essential oils by diffusing them, ingesting them, and including them in homemade soaps, deodorants and other products. I personally know doctors who prescribe them as an alternative to medicine. While the allopathic (conventional) medical approach is sometimes needed, the use of herbs, essential oils and healing foods have helped numerous people clear up chronic illness without the use of synthetic, manufactured medicines that often have very negative side effects because they do not work with our body's natural chemistry.

Essential oils are especially powerful because you will receive the benefits of hundreds of plants in one drop. They are extracted from various parts of the plant or tree, which can include the bark, root, flower, seed, or fruit. Use a therapeutic-grade essential oil rather than the cheapest oil you can find, because some of these brands may use chemicals to extract the oil from the plant. I have many, many essential oils and oil blends in my medicine cabinet at home, and because of their high quality and potency, I can often feel the effects within minutes of using them. Oils can be taken internally, topically or through diffusion, depending upon the oil. Experiment with different ones to see what works best for you. Many of them have multiple uses, so you get your money's worth from these little bottles.

I have known people to use herbs and essential oils to create their own cleaning and beauty products, to ward off illness, cure digestive distress, help them sleep better, and quell anxiety. I love the warm, soothing nature of herbal tea, which I also use for healing. For example, mint is good for soothing digestive distress, valerian for calming the mind, and milk thistle for detoxifying the liver. The herbs you find in teas can often be found in essential oil or tincture form as well. I enjoy using a mix of teas, tinctures and oils for therapeutic use.

Eat authentic food

Processed foods are full of chemicals, such as artificial flavors and colors that are unnatural and therefore do not work naturally with your body. They are also high in cheap forms of sodium and hidden sugars, which can cause you to retain water and gain weight, and have a profound effect on your blood sugar and mood, dimming your inner light. Buy a glucose monitoring kit if you are concerned about blood sugar or are known to get "hangry." I stopped having "hangry" episodes when I cut out processed foods, including all flour-based foods. Now, I get hungry like a normal person! High or low blood glucose could be connected to mood, and some experts argue that eating a plate of pasta or rice can have a greater impact on blood sugar than regular table sugar! I have definitely found that to be the case, even with brown rice or gluten-free pasta. This doesn't mean you have to give these items up completely, but eat them sparingly, and keep track of how different foods impact your digestion, energy level and mood. We are all different, which means one person's pleasure could be another person's poison.

It is crucial that the first meal of the day is a healthy one full of good protein sources, fiber, vitamins, minerals and healthy

fats. This sets the stage for how the rest of the day is going to play out. If you eat breakfast cereal full of sugar, you will probably have a blood sugar spike followed by a crash later in the morning, causing you to reach for yet another cup of coffee and to eat a heavier lunch, perhaps loaded with carbs for quick energy. When you go for a high-carb lunch, especially a refined carb lunch, this will cause another spike and another crash, leading to the strong urge to grab a sugary snack at about 3 P.M. and perhaps yet another cup of coffee. This could also lead to mood swings, exhaustion, and episodes of being "hangry." By the time you return home, you probably won't feel like exercising, meditating, creating, or any of the other things that make you whole and lead you to soul. Instead, you will be tempted to reach for a beer or glass of wine and veg in front of the TV to unwind. This is a vicious cycle that all started when you woke up in the morning and provided your body with inefficient fuel. Throughout the day, think about providing your body with premium fuel versus fuel with lots of fillers and empty calories. Your food talks to your genes, and all of this affects your emotional state, cognitive ability and energy levels.

Do a cleanse

By consuming cleansing foods and herbs and engaging in intermittent fasting and other cleansing activities, you can start purging your body of toxins and clearing your mind, allowing room for spirit to enter. When I cleanse, I quickly lose any extra weight I've been carrying around, mostly around my belly, and feel lighter in both body and spirit. My digestive distress calms, and my energy increases. Our brain is part of our body, and when we clear the toxins from our body, this vital part of our body is included! When you

cleanse your body and mind, you sleep better, digest food better, have more energy, and respond to stress better. You also open yourself up to greater awareness and expanded consciousness.

The cleanses I guide my clients through are at least twenty-one days, but if this is too daunting for you, dip your toe into the water of cleansing by cleaning up your diet. Can you go two weeks or more with no processed sugars and refined carbs? Can you cut out dairy for two to three weeks and then add it back in to see how you feel? Perhaps you can tolerate cultured dairy, such as yogurt, but have difficulty with regular milk. What about trying the same experiment with gluten? Try drinking warm water with lemon first thing in the morning or in the evening. For an additional boost, one of my friends likes adding apple cider vinegar. When I work with clients, I first have them incorporate more cleansing herbal teas and foods into their diet and slowly increase the intensity of the detoxification process. Start where you feel comfortable. We are all exposed to so many toxins that are products of the modern world, but are unnatural to our ancient DNA, that our bodies often need extra help ridding itself of these chemicals. Our bodies have a built-in system for detoxification, but this system can become overloaded, and some people's bodies are better at taking out the trash than others. Toxins can make us feel sluggish and sick, blocking our creativity and access to spirit.

Music and digestion

Turn off the TV and tune in to music while eating. Find pieces of music that relax your mind and body. Have you ever noticed that you get indigestion if you eat while under stress? When we eat while in flight or fight mode, our sympathetic

nervous system responds to that stress by slowing digestion and putting on fat, particularly around the middle, to build up reserves to live on during what it perceives to be an emergency situation. Having extra fat signals the body to store even more fat, creating a vicious snowball effect. By listening to relaxing music and engaging in deep breathing, you are eliciting a response from the parasympathetic nervous system, which calms you down and tells the body you are no longer in danger. If you are focusing on incorporating healthier foods into your diet, experiment to see if associating these relaxing tunes with what you are eating makes you want these foods when you listen to the same music in the future. What songs or types of music do you associate with which foods? I often associate pasta and wine with certain classical pieces, so if I'm trying to cut down on these foods, I might listen to more meditative tunes, such as Carlos Nakai playing the Native American cedar flute. When I listen to Native American music, I picture oneness with and respect for nature, and so I don't feel compelled to overeat. Experiment to find what works for you!

Your Brain on Food

I recently did a Facebook poll to find out how foods affected my friends on a physical, cognitive, and emotional level. Many reported that fried foods made them feel lethargic and lowered their ability to concentrate. A large percentage reported that veggies and green juices made them feel clear-headed, light and focused. When I consume certain adaptagenic herbs, I feel happy and inspired. (Adaptagenic herbs adapt to the needs of your body. For example, these herbs can raise blood pressure in a person whose level is too low, but lower it in someone whose blood pressure is too

high). When I eat ghee and warming spices, such as cinnamon, I feel more grounded. If I eat refined carbs, I have an energy crash, leaving me feeling lethargic, apathetic and unproductive. My blood sugar then dips too low, leaving me feeling out of control emotionally.

An important part of understanding the food-mood connection is exploring your cravings. If you are craving chocolate, for example, you could have a magnesium deficiency, or the taste could remind you of drinking hot chocolate in the dorm room with your best friend that you have been thinking about and missing recently. There is always a life-affirming reason behind our cravings, even if the craving doesn't seem healthy. For example, when exploring her craving for a popular hamburger chain, which she knew wasn't healthy, my client realized the food reminded her of her childhood, when life was easier and simpler. By understanding the origin of the craving, she was able to satisfy her craving in a healthier way. She bought grass-fed ground beef and made her own hamburgers at home instead. By being consciously aware of our cravings and understanding where they are coming from, we can give our minds, bodies, and spirits what they need, but in a healthier way.

Our cravings are more likely to surface when we are stressed. For many of us, stress is such a constant companion, we hardly even notice its presence except through the awareness of our cravings. One of my clients noticed that she craved sweet foods when stressed and crunchy foods, like potato chips, when bored, which is another form of stress. She also noticed that she sometimes felt hungry when she was actually dehydrated!

Sometimes a sugar craving is a sign you need more sweetness

in your life. Perhaps a hug from a friend or some deep breathing would ease the craving. Maybe you are low on energy due to dehydration, lack of sufficient sleep, or the high-carb meal you had for lunch. Can you replace your cravings with a healthier alternative? Try taking a brisk walk, relaxing in the sun, or having a cup of green tea. Keep a food journal to see if you can start seeing patterns. Although cravings often point to a nutritional deficiency, you may be surprised to find that many of your cravings stem from the need to return to the authenticity of the spirit. Cravings are signposts that point us in the direction of what we need to thrive and be happy. Embrace them and learn from them.

Chapter 4 ~ Walk the Path:

1. Experiment with herbs and spices. Note changes in mood, digestion, body temperature, and overall well-being in your journal. For high-quality herbs and spices, visit www.mountainroseherbs.com.
2. Find out your primary dosha, and spend a week engaging in eating foods and making lifestyle changes according to your dosha. Note any changes you see.
3. Develop a ritual for at least one of your meals. Perhaps you eat lunch outside in nature during your lunch hour instead of at your desk or enjoy dinner with candles and music instead of on the couch in front of the TV.
4. Plant a small garden, even if it's an indoor one, and use what you produce when preparing meals.
5. Start creating positive memories with healthier foods, such as bringing a raw pie with lower sugar to holiday dinners, having friends over for a vegan pot luck once a month, or reading a few pages out of an inspirational book each morning with a cup of herbal tea.
6. Keep a food journal. This is one of the most powerful tools I use with my clients. Note any patterns you see. Sometimes food reactions can be delayed a few days or even a week.

Chapter 5

The Warrior Path ~ Train like a Ninja

"Life is like riding a bicycle. To keep your balance, you must keep moving." ~ Albert Einstein

"He who conquers others is strong. He who conquers himself is mighty." Lao Tsu

When I picture a ninja warrior, I imagine someone who is strong, swift, flexible, graceful and clear-headed all at the same time. The warrior is dedicated to eating healthy foods that build muscle and clear the body of toxins. The warrior also takes time to sleep, meditate and reflect, allowing internal balance and resilience. This person is in "flow" with the surrounding world and moves through it effortlessly. In addition to taking care of our bodies and minds, we must also choose the right form of movement. It must be an activity we feel inspired to do that is also well-suited to our temperament. Since much of athletic performance is mental as well as physical, we must also train our minds to be strong and flexible.

Be challenged and be present

Athletes are excellent warriors. When I watch Yu-na Kim on the ice, I am always amazed at her composure as she lands perfect jumps, demonstrates flawless footwork, and spins with beauty, grace and control. In addition to skating in front of millions of people in one of the most competitive events in the world, she also has the national pride of her country on her shoulders. During one of her performances, one of the commentators explained that as a Korean, her successes equal

success for the whole nation. If she fails, it is seen as a national failure.

I was nervous weeks before my first ice-skating test. Every time I thought about it, my heart beat faster, and I felt a rush of blood in my veins. During practice, my coach was often frustrated with the fact that I was still struggling with details that could be my demise in front of the judges. Each morning of practice, I stepped out on the ice at 6 A.M. This means I dragged myself out of bed at 4:30 A.M. After skating for an hour, I quickly dashed off to a high-stress job managing more than twenty employees. On the days I worked with my coach, I didn't even have time to warm up because my lesson started right at 6 A.M. Since that was the earliest anyone was allowed on the ice, I had to do the moves "cold," which allowed my weaknesses to be fully revealed. She reminded me that the judges would be able to hear every scratch of my toe pick and would be judging me for both power and technical ability. The whole process was daunting, but at least I didn't have the pressure of Yu-na Kim.

Although I spent hours upon hours in practice, much of my preparation was mental. I was studying to be a HeartMath® coach at the time, so I incorporated a few techniques from that program during my practice, including breathing through my heart to stay present and to disengage from any negative thoughts that might arise. Time and time again, my ego whined, "What if I fall on the *easy* parts? I will look like such a fool! What if I catch an edge? What if I fail the test? All of my friends will know and my coach will be disappointed." Each time, I brought the attention back to my breath and told my little child of an ego that everything would be okay: there is a part of me that is eternal and cannot be destroyed no matter

what happens in this life. I drew upon my yoga training to coordinate each breath with my moves, which again caused me to focus on the present moment rather than the scary next move. A fellow skater advised me to think about the three things I needed to do for each move prior to doing the move. These should be the main components I needed to do to execute the move appropriately. My coach advised me to visualize myself going through each move of the test before I got out of bed each morning. This way, I would mentally rehearse my program when my brain was more relaxed and less critical. As I mentioned in other chapters, the morning is a magical time for meditation and creativity. It is also a great time for transformation and for returning to the divine within.

I did this mental preparation along with many hours of hard practice during the busiest time of the year at my job. I showed up for the test two hours early to warm up and get focused. During the test, I was only slightly nervous. If anything, I felt inspired and joyful, and I did better on the test than I did in practice! Practice and mental preparation are most effective when we incorporate focusing on the present moment, coordinate our movements with our breath, and maintain awareness of the indestructible spirit within.

Do what you love and watch your spirit fly

Although I am an ice skater now, I never once skated as a kid, but it was something I had always wanted to try. Where I grew up, there was no rink nearby, but perhaps the biggest reason I never skated was fear due to the story of my great-grandmother gradually going blind from the age of sixteen due to an ice skating-accident. My mom enrolled me in gymnastics instead, which I loved. I enjoyed the power and flexibility required, and I was good at it. I loved practicing my

walkovers and handsprings over and over and over until they were perfect. Then I stopped taking gymnastics, probably because the school where I took lessons stopped giving them. Life went on. I slowly stopped practicing and tried to find enjoyment in "regular" sports offered by my school.

One of those sports was track, which I started in middle school. All of my family members were runners: parents, brother, sisters, cousins and uncles. Drive down our road at any given point in the day, and whether the weather is rainy, snowy or hot and humid, you'll find one of my family members running. In high school, I ran the 400-meter dash and the 1600-meter relay (another 400-meter dash). While I was good at it, and I loved the bonding experience and life lessons it taught, I didn't *love* the act of running. I enjoyed it once I got past the side-stitch-nausea phase of being out of shape, but beyond track season, I didn't keep up with running on a regular basis, especially once I reached college and beyond. I ran sporadically because I just wasn't inspired. My dad and his brothers, on the other hand, have been life-long runners. My dad used to get up every morning at 6 A.M. to run 6 miles before heading off to work. My uncle is so addicted to running that when he had to temporarily stop due to tendonitis, he nearly went stir crazy. I never loved running that much. I wanted to love running, but I just didn't. I only *liked* running, so I often found myself falling off the exercise wagon.

When I analyzed why I didn't stick to my running routine, I realized that it sometimes put me in an aggressive state. I often became overheated while running in warmer weather, and the intensity exacerbated my already high levels of stress. When I discovered ice skating at age thirty-eight, my world

changed. The cool air of the rink has a calming effect, even though I still work up a sweat. I never overheat, so my mind stays calm as well. It is intense, but in bursts of intensity. I skate, jump, land and prep for the next jump. It takes lots and lots of practice, so there is always something to work towards and to improve. It also takes full concentration, putting me in a meditative state. I love the music, the feeling of flying when I'm on the ice, and the beauty, grace, strength, power, and creativity required for the sport. I'd always loved watching figure skating during the Winter Olympics, and now here I was, out there learning the various jumps, spins and moves on the ice. When I'm skating, I'm more than an athlete. I'm an artist.

Finding something you love that has a positive effect on your psyche is huge. If pumping iron at the gym is something you do because you "should," rather than because it's what really motivates you, then you might want to consider finding a different form of exercise, or at least one that will motivate you to go to the gym for cross training. Dancing is a great workout, as is playing basketball or soccer, mountain biking, hiking, martial arts, gardening and even housekeeping. There are many, many ways to incorporate movement into your life, so pick one or two activities you love and form a community around them. Your soul will thank you.

Warrior Pack

I've made many friends at the rink, and I am part of a community of adult skaters who share my passion for the sport. People are pack animals at heart rather than lone wolves, and so although I'm an introvert, I am much more inspired and courageous when I skate with friends. We give each other tips, commiserate when we have a bad fall or can't

land a jump, and celebrate each other's successes.

My Uncle Phil, who I mentioned earlier, has been a runner his entire life. He has run five Boston Marathons, one New York Marathon, and numerous others. He even ran a marathon in just under a six-minute pace. I've never even run one mile that quickly, and he did it for over twenty-six miles! Although I'm sure he has some genetic mutation that allows him to do this, he credits his "tribe" for his success and ability to stick with running for so many years. As a physical education minor in college, he learned that doing a sport with three to four people rather than just yourself or one other person greatly increases its effectiveness. Although he is sixty-five, you can still spot my Uncle Phil running up and down the road with his tribe.

Exercise and your dosha

In Ayurveda, practitioners stress the importance of doing the right kind of exercise for your dosha, or constitution. The three doshas, as mentioned in the previous chapter, are vata, pitta and kapha. Kaphas, for example, who are normally bigger, more athletic in build, and have a calmer temperament, will benefit from more intense exercise, such as running. Pittas, on the other hand, who are fiery, intense and driven, benefit from slower, calmer forms of exercise, such as Tai Chi or yoga. One of my friends, who is a vata and tends to get cold easily, loves running in the heat. It makes me miserable. Find an activity that balances you. For example, if you are naturally passive, then more intense activities will bring you into balance. If you are naturally intense, then consider incorporating gentler activities to help balance you. When we have too much of one thing, it can cause both physical and mental imbalances. Also honor that you are in a

constant state of flux, and more intense exercise may benefit you more at certain times of the day or year than others. In the fall and winter, my vata tends to be higher, so warming exercises, such as warm vinyasa flow (yoga), work better for me at this time of year than during summer when my "pitta" tends to be higher.

My husband's granddad was a fighter pilot for the Royal Air Force during World War II and later moved his family from England to New Braunfels, Texas, which is a small town situated on a spring-fed river. In his forties, he started swimming in that river every morning as a way to manage stress. He would probably be swimming today if the river hadn't started to dry up, making it too shallow to swim. When he was younger, he was also known for taking long walks in the wilderness by himself. He would be gone for days. These were forms of activities that he not only loved, but that he also found calming.

What works for one person may not work for another, so find what works for your constitution. I have a friend and personal trainer who loves rock climbing. One of my clients lives for her gym workout. These activities do not speak to me, and what does speak to me depends on my level of stress at the time. Skating and swimming are both great activities for me during high-stress periods because they don't cause me to overheat. Overheating causes a negative psycho-somatic reaction, resulting in responses such as aggression. If you are like me, this doesn't mean you shouldn't do high intensity exercise, but just be careful about the level of intensity, your emotional state when doing it, and the temperature in which you are doing the activity. Note how your form of exercise affects you mentally. I love skating for the qualities

mentioned above and swimming for its cooling, meditative, repetitive nature. When I get out of the pool, I feel like my whole body has had a massage. It works muscles that other sports do not, and it's easy on my joints.

Flexibility and mental strength

Yoga is a great way to unwind and learn to let go to be in flow, and there are so many forms of it out there, there's a style that's sure to suit everyone. For example, vinyasa is a "stronger" form of yoga during which one flows from one pose to the next and it is sometimes done in a heated room. Restorative yoga, on the other hand, is a calmer form that uses props to help deepen the poses. In Yin yoga, students hold each pose for minutes at a time, stretching the fascia surrounding the muscles instead of merely stretching the muscles. Yoga is my medication, and I'm not in balance if I don't do it daily. In fact, if I skip more than one day in a row, I am more likely to get in touch with my mental demons rather than my soul! Yoga helps get rid of the physical tightness left over from sleep that could potentially turn into mental tightness during the day. I do it first thing in the morning, followed by meditation and reading from a spiritual text. Although it's a great way to begin the new day, many find benefit from doing yoga in the evenings to release the tension from the day.

If yoga seems too intimidating, try doing a private one-to-one session with a yoga instructor before taking a class, or try Tai Chi. It is a gentler, slower form of movement and is a beautiful practice. When I visited Vietnam, I remember walking down the beach one morning and seeing numerous agile elderly people doing the slow, graceful movements of Tai Chi along the boardwalk at sunrise. Many hospitals and

adult education programs have Tai Chi classes for seniors, but anyone at any age can benefit. Because the movement is so slow and focused, the mind also has to slow down and be present, which is great mental training for sitting meditation or for the overactive mind.

The martial arts require flexibility, strength and great mental discipline for the warrior within. There are many forms of martial arts. Like yoga, if you search, you are likely to find a form that fits with your philosophy and style. Knowing that you could defend yourself, if necessary, allows you to be more comfortable in your own skin and less on edge as you move through life. One of the members of my networking group has studied karate for more than twenty years. He walks with confidence and ease through the world because he knows he can handle any situation that comes his way. He can not only protect himself, but also those he loves. This confidence carries over into everyday activities, such as dealing with potential clients and giving presentations. He exudes confidence and stability, even when under pressure.

Strength building

In addition to aerobic activity, such as hiking and swimming, and working on flexibility through activities such as yoga, be sure to include resistance training or strength training. This mimics the manual labor our ancestors had to do, which is more natural than sitting at a desk all day. Unfortunately, working from a desk is what so many of us must do to earn a living, so we have to make a concerted effort to engage in activities that were a normal part of the lives of our ancestors. It doesn't have to be difficult, though. In fact, you can do strength training at your office. Do push-ups on the floor or against a wall. You can also do squats, toe raises, standing leg

lifts, lunges and many other activities. This will give you a burst of energy and make that extra cup of coffee less tempting. The good news is that you don't have to do this all at once. If you don't have an hour to set aside for exercise, do little bits throughout the day. Some experts claim this is better than sitting all day and then doing an hour of exercise anyway. Cleaning house, raking leaves, and gardening are wonderful, natural ways to increase strength, so don't neglect your chores!

Interval Training

Be sure to include some interval training with either your aerobic workout or strength training workout. It helps you handle stress, can be done in just a few minutes, and will add power to your workout. For example, try jumping rope or running in place as quickly as you can for thirty seconds, then go at about half speed for a minute, then go full speed for another thirty, half speed for one minute, etc until you have done at least four rounds. You can also do this as a stand-alone activity if you are in a rush and don't have time for anything else. If you are a runner, you can incorporate sprints into your workout, for example. That way, you are combining aerobic and interval training.

Take care of this once-in-an-eternity body

Exercise is crucial for stress management and a healthy body. Your eternal soul resides temporarily within the body. This body allows the soul to experience the world of matter, but it's hard to truly experience the world if we are tired, weak or ill. Your body, this form to which your soul is currently attached, will never be seen again. It is precious. Be sure to give it the best life it can have by incorporating some movement, even if

only a handful of minutes, each day. Make it your goal to do twenty to forty minutes daily and to work up a sweat, but remember, something is much better than nothing at all. Even if you are exhausted when you come home from work, and exercising is the last thing on your mind, force yourself to change into your workout clothes before sitting down to rest or eating a snack. Do interval training or strength training, or go for a short walk. No matter how tired I was after work, I always felt more energized after doing even a little bit of exercising and I never regretted doing it.

Find a routine that works and stick to it. I know that Monday, Wednesday and Saturday, I'm going to the rink to skate. It is part of my routine. For yoga, I don't even leave my house. I just do it at home each morning upon waking. If I don't do it first, I don't do it. On the days I don't go to the rink, I do strength training or go for a hike. One of my clients works out at lunch, and another one exercises immediately after work. Know thyself. Do what works for you. If one routine doesn't work, keep trying different things until you find one that does. It's worth it.

The psychology and spirit of movement

Movement can be much more meaningful if you incorporate mental strength training and spiritual development into your routine. As you run, imagine you are a deer swiftly running through the forest. As you are jumping rope, feel the strong beat of your heart as it helps your body release mental and physical toxins. As you do yoga, focus on the body and breath becoming one.

If you are a competitive athlete and find yourself having anxiety about your upcoming marathon or dance

performance, visualize the place you will be performing. Imagine that space being completely filled with yellow light, pink bubbles, or whatever resonates with you. The space is so completely filled, there is no room for negativity. You can do this visualization between waking and sleeping, but you can also do it while you are practicing in the recital hall or running with your team. During your competition or performance, imagine yourself surrounded and protected by this light. Focus on coordinating your breath with your movement, as we discussed in the chapter on breath and meditation. Breathe deeply and rhythmically. Imagine all tension draining out of your arms and legs as you inhale healing light and exhale it back to everyone and everything around you.

In a journal, keep track of how different forms of movement, the time of day you do these activities, and the conditions in which you do them, affect your energy levels and emotions. In addition to helping you build strength, flexibility and resilience, and to release toxins from the body, movement should also help you release mental and emotional toxins. These combined benefits enable you to achieve balance and freedom from the harmful effects of everyday stress. During your practice, work on incorporating breath work, flexibility, mental strength, and spiritual connection. A gym workout can be a superficial act of pumping iron to look better at the beach or part of a spiritual quest for wholeness and realized potential. It's all in your approach.

Chapter 5 ~ Walk the Path

1. What physical activities did you love as a kid? Revisit this activity or an "adult" form of it. Maybe you can't do gymnastics anymore, but yoga might be a good alternative. Did you play basketball? Find an adult intramural team.
2. Try something new, even if it frightens you. Did you always want to be a ballerina? The next American Ninja? Take an adult ballet class or find a rock climbing gym to try.
3. Push yourself a bit further in your current activity. Add a mile to your usual bike ride. See if you can add five more pushups. Swim for an extra ten minutes. Imagine your body as already strong, healed and whole.
4. Create ways to incorporate mind, body and spirit with your chosen form of movement. Before skating, I incorporate breath work, interval training and stretching or yoga. When I'm on the ice, I coordinate my breath with each step, allowing greater mental focus. I imagine the other skaters and myself enveloped in healing light and feel my spirit taking flight as I glide or push off of the ice. I give silent thanks for the freedom and health to participate in this activity, even though it scares me. I know the soul likes risk, because risk allows growth.
5. Join a group to walk this path with you or form one yourself.

Chapter 6

The Path of Restoration – The Beauty of Rest and Sleep

"In man's dream-consciousness, where he has loosened in his sleep his clutch on the egoistic limitations that daily hem him round, the omnipotence of his mind has a nightly demonstration. Lo! There in the dream stand the long-dead friends, the remotest continents, the resurrected scenes of his childhood." ~ Paramhansa Yogananda, from Autobiography of a Yogi

The land of dreams is mysterious, bringing us to the border of life and death, a land of fairy tales and magic. Lucid dreaming is one of the many fascinating aspects of this elusive world, and most people have done it at least once. I first formally learned about lucid dreaming from a student I was teaching. I noticed he kept looking at his watch, and I asked him if he was bored. "No," he responded. "I was doing a reality check." Upon seeing my look of confusion, he explained that he routinely did reality checks by looking at a watch or clock to determine whether or not he was dreaming. When you look at a clock in a dream, he explained, it often didn't have a face or any numbers. If he was dreaming, he wanted to know so he could control it.

He had just spent a few months out in the woods living out of a tent, cooking his own food over a fire, and learning how to be aware he was dreaming while he was asleep. When you become aware of the fact you are dreaming, you can experience anything you desire. In his dreams, he enjoyed flying. I was blown away by this and decided to try it myself. It took some time and practice, but I was able to do it. It was

exhilarating! I decided to fly, and while I was dreaming, I felt completely awake. That's what makes lucid dreaming so powerful. You can control it and it feels completely *real.* When I told one of my closest friends about my experiment, she told me she learned to lucid dream in order to stop having nightmares when she was younger. She loves sleep and the magic of dreams.

Sleep is a time for the body to heal and rebuild itself, burn fat, process the day's events, solve problems and fully engage in the creative process. Do everything you can to prevent the disruption of these important nocturnal events! I once dreamed about watching a woman play a song on the piano I had been trying to figure out by ear. In the dream, I saw the pattern and remembered it upon waking. I was able to sit down and play this piece on the piano as a result of the dream. If we don't sleep properly, we may have difficulty reaching this creative dream stage. Many people would argue that sleeping and dreams are an important part of spiritual development. So how do we turn off our thinking brains in order get our dose of this nocturnal medicine and tune in to its messages?

The brain that won't be still

Like many people with over-active brains, I have had a history of insomnia. This can result from many causes. Sometimes there's more than one cause at a time for a tough night's sleep and the causes may vary from night to night. Some people have trouble falling asleep, like my husband. They keep thinking about the day's events, especially work-related ones and have a tough time calming down enough to begin the sleep cycle. I've never had difficulty falling asleep. I'm so

active during the day, that after a few minutes of reading, I fall asleep easily. In spite of this, I would often wake up at 3:00 A.M., convinced it was 6:00 A.M., which was my normal wake-up time. I felt totally awake when this happened and rarely fell back asleep. According to Dr. Mark Hyman, "The two MOST common culprits threatening your sleep wake cycles are unregulated blood sugar levels or poor nutrition status and chronic stress." According to the various Traditional Chinese Medicine Practitioners and acupuncturists I visited regarding the problem, I had stagnant liver chi. My chiropractor told me it was due to a deficiency in the neurotransmitter GABA. Knowing that they were all probably right, I took several actions to help me get a better night's sleep and have listed some of them below.

Ease your digestion

Sometimes poor sleep is due to poor digestion, especially if you are waking up in the middle of the sleep cycle like I am. I have a history of digestive issues, which is one of the reasons I decided to study nutrition and become an integrative nutrition coach. I now know what upsets my stomach and when I digest food best. Peak digestion times tend to be from ten in the morning to two or three in the afternoon. From an ayurvedic standpoint, this is when "pitta" is strongest. Pitta is related to fire, including digestive fire. My digestion becomes weaker in the evening, so it's not ideal for me to eat anything after 7 P.M. Try eating your highest protein meals for breakfast and lunch and eat a smaller, easier-to-digest meal for dinner. While I *love* raw foods, including a good raw salad at lunch, I tend to prefer steamed veggies at dinner and fish for protein over beans, nuts or seeds since the latter three are harder to digest. I save those for the ten to three period.

Crock-pot meals can also be great dinners, since they basically cook themselves all day, and the food is softer, more tender and easier to digest.

Another way to improve digestion is to take digestive enzymes and to eat probiotic foods, such as sauerkraut, with your meals to aid digestion. (The sauerkraut or fermented veggies are usually in the vegan "meat" section of a health food store. The gray stuff you put on hot dogs doesn't count). If you have "leaky gut," you will want to avoid gluten, dairy, and most nuts, seeds and beans for awhile since these are all difficult to digest. Your stomach needs time to heal. I use a wonderful essential oil blend specifically to stimulate digestion that is also very soothing to my sensitive stomach.

If you have poor "digestive fire" or low stomach acid, you can talk to a holistic doctor about taking hydrochloric acid, which is essentially stomach acid, to help you digest your meals. Some experts argue that this is not a good long-term solution, though, and that a better long-term solution is consuming bitters, such as ginger, gentian root, goldenseal root, Oregon burdock root, and dandelion root. When consumed as a tea, dandelion root tastes similar to coffee. You can also buy premade Swedish bitters at a health food store. Bitters have been used by other cultures for years to stimulate digestion. There are many causes of low stomach acid, and among those causes is chronic stress. By doing the activities in this book to manage stress, you might also improve your digestion!

Actively manage your stress before bed time

Here's an activity you can do at the end of the day to help with sleep. Stress tends to accumulate throughout the day unless we do something about it. When I was being trained as

a coach in the HeartMath® technique, I learned that it's not the big stressors that usually get us, but what my coach called "the ankle biters." These are the tiny little stressors throughout the day that, by themselves, are not a big deal. Add them together at the end of the day, and you'll understand why you are wiped out. In fact, many people have so many of these little stressors prior to making it out the door for work that they are exhausted by the time they reach the office. Learn to recognize stress in your body more quickly, and then take steps to mitigate its effects. One thing you can do is turn the negative view of the stressful event into a positive. For example, if you are late to work because your child refused to eat her breakfast, perhaps this was a message. Maybe her behavior is hinting at a food allergy or sensitivity. Perhaps she is struggling in school and is sick to her stomach about the possibility of being called on to read aloud in class. Or maybe she just wanted to spend an extra few minutes with you. There is yin and yang, shadow and light, in everything. We are great at looking at the shadow side, but what is the situation bringing to light?

You can also take stock at the end of the day. Think about all of those little stressors, including negative thoughts, that you didn't mitigate during the day. How can you turn those into positives? After doing this activity, take several slow, deep breaths and think about all that you have to be grateful for until you are able to actually *feel* a sense of gratitude, even if it's just for being able to sit and breathe for a few quiet moments. Doing this will have a drastic impact on your mood, your overall health, and your ability to sleep well at night.

Stay cool

People often have difficulty sleeping when the season becomes warmer and the air conditioners have not been turned on yet. I recently felt freezing cold upon going to bed, so I turned up the electric blanket to the highest setting . . . and then fell asleep. I woke up sweating in the middle of the night and had restless sleep the rest of the night, even after turning off the blanket and cooling down. If you are going to use your electric blanket, be sure to turn it OFF before falling asleep. You can also take a warm bath followed by a cool blast of water before going to bed. This act of getting warm and then rapidly cooling off can induce sleep. Keep your thermostat low – I keep mine between sixty-four to sixty-seven degrees Fahrenheit – and you will not only sleep better, but save money on the heating bill. I also like to slightly crack the window, even in winter, to get cool, fresh air into the room.

In the evening, live like the Amish

Being active well into the evening is a recipe for poor sleep. Add artificial light to the scene, and this compounds the issue. Cut off the use of bright, overhead lights and electronics at least a couple of hours before bed time. This includes watching TV, checking email on your phone, or surfing the net on your computer. (No, you don't need a TV in your room. Keep your bedroom for sex and sleep. That's it.) Be sure you also finish your exercise routine, stop working, finish dinner and complete your chores prior to this time. Do these things earlier in the evening, and use the last two hours to do more relaxing activities, such as reading, knitting, building a model airplane, playing games with your kids or your pets, playing a musical instrument or some other creative/relaxing activity. Evening can be magical if you turn off the noise and turn

down the lights. Read under a lamp instead of a bright overhead light. I like to write in the evening by the light of a Tiffany-style lamp and large candle. Even though it can be a huge challenge to get everything done two hours before bed, which means 8 P.M. for me, the rewards are worth it. I'm able to take time to slow down, reflect on the day, decompress from the day's stressors, and tune in to my creativity when I stick to this routine. Then I can accomplish even more the next day because I've slept well and have taken the time to nourish myself from within.

Examine your cortisol addiction

Some hyperactive people now label themselves "cortisol junkies." They thrive on stress, on doing, on the go-go-go. It took me a LONG time to admit this, but I don't like going to sleep. I'd rather be awake so I can learn, grow, heal myself, heal others, create, and live life. I love life, and sleep is a kind of death for me. Rationally, I know I will die sooner if I don't get adequate sleep. I also know that I will be much less effective and less creative if I'm not well-rested, but I have a difficult time accepting this emotionally. This is why I find lucid dreaming so alluring. Create a ritual around sleep that makes it something you look forward to rather than dread. Reward yourself for having the discipline to follow the other steps. Start a dream journal or learn to lucid dream in order to see the value in sleeping.

Cut the caffeine and go for protein

For some people, drinking coffee can trigger a flight-or-fight response. For this reason, coffee is not allowed during the cleanse period with my clients. When your body is in flight-or-fight mode, it stores fat to get you through the perceived

emergency. Cortisol and adrenaline levels rise, storing fat around your belly. Some people are more sensitive to caffeine than others and may not expel caffeine from their systems as efficiently, allowing the drug to stay in their bodies for several hours longer than the average person. Instead, try green tea for awhile to see if that helps, and avoid consuming caffeine after lunch.

Also, be careful about what you eat in the evening. Try a meal with good quality protein that is low in carbs and contains calcium and magnesium. Wild-caught salmon with brussels sprouts or adzuki beans and butternut squash are some examples. The protein will help you control blood sugar and stay satiated so you don't wake up hungry. If you are deficient in magnesium, this may result in nervousness and insomnia. Calcium deficiency could result in muscle cramps and other issues. Although cacao is a good source of magnesium and other minerals, you might want to avoid this at dinner time, as it also contains stimulants. (This is a great excuse to eat dark chocolate during the day, though! Just make sure that you get products that are *at least* 70% cacao).

Restorative Yoga On and Off the Matt

One of the poses I remember from restorative yoga classes that helped me relax involved lying on my back and putting the backs of my legs and butt against the wall, forming an "L" shape with my body. You can use this pose before going to bed to help you fall asleep. If you are already in bed and are struggling to go back to sleep, lie on your back and bring feet wide with the soles of your feet on the mattress. Then let your knees fall toward one another, forming a tent shape. This releases the lower back. Another pose you can do in bed is to lie on your back, soles of feet together and knees wide, making

a diamond shape with your legs, which opens up the hips. We store lots of tension in our hips, so hip openers such as this one can be surprisingly relaxing. I have often fallen back asleep by using this pose.

Take a break

Take time to rest throughout the day and week. It will be easier to unwind at night. Plan a vacation or staycation. Just the act of planning a relaxing vacation can make you feel better. You will be able to see light at the end of the tunnel and get out of the rut of the day-to-day. Try taking a cat nap in the middle of the day. When I was a busy director and needed a little nap, I would set an alarm on my phone for twenty minutes and take a nap in my car. More than that amount usually made me feel groggy, and I didn't have that much time anyway. Take a leisurely stroll after lunch or go sit in a park. Consider dropping in on a restorative yoga class after work or on the weekend.

Use a little sorcery

Okay, that might be a bit exaggerated. In all seriousness, great healers and shamen have used herbs to cure people for centuries. There are sleep tonics, essential oils, and teas you can use to help you fall asleep and stay asleep. If that doesn't help, you should consider getting tested through a holistic doctor to see if you are low on any of the neurotransmitters. When I spoke with my chiropractor about my incredibly challenging sleep issues, she suggested I try taking the neurotransmitter, GABA, to calm me down when I felt mentally wired. Because she is a doctor, she has access to higher-quality "potions" that you can't get over the counter. It worked like a charm. In addition to the previously-mentioned

suggestions, I use GABA in combination with an herbal detoxifying strip I wear over my liver. After over a decade of waking up in the middle of the night and being unable to fall back asleep, I now have become a sleeping beauty rather a sleep-deprived hag!

Chapter 6 ~ Walk the Path

1. Try taking a warm, detoxifying bath before bed. Make sure the water is warm, but not hot. Add a cup or two of Epsom salts and several drops of lavender essential oil.
2. Meditate and practice deep breathing about an hour before bedtime.
3. Read a calming, spiritual text before going to sleep.
4. Dim the lights and turn off all electronics two hours before bedtime one evening. Note the results.
5. Keep a sleep and dream journal. Write down the time you went to bed, how well you slept, and any dreams you had.
6. Attend a restorative yoga class.

Chapter 7

The Path of Dharma – Find Your True Calling

"Everyone is a genius, but if you judge a fish on its ability to climb a tree, it will live its whole life believing it is stupid." ~ Albert Einstein

"Do not be too timid and squeamish about your actions. All life is an experiment." Ralph Waldo Emerson

I attended graduate school in Durham, England. Surrounded by piles of books and intellectuals from all over the world who had converged in this quaint English town, I felt at home. When I walked across the old bridges that stretched across the river Weir or looked up at the Gothic cathedral whose spires were enveloped in mist, I felt inspired. On a daily basis, I sat with my fellow students in our kitchen, drank tea, and discussed European politics, literature, and art. My "job" was to read volumes of books and synthesize this information into numerous essays and eventually a dissertation. I loved it.

When I finished my degree, I was determined to find something that felt like graduate school, so I decided to go into publishing. I had a hard time finding work, as many recent graduates do. I wanted to stay in England and tried desperately to convince companies to hire me, even though it meant taking the expensive and unnecessary step of paying for my visa. Since there were plenty of British nationals with English degrees looking for positions, I was unsuccessful. I moved to Boston, but found that the publishing companies paid poorly, especially when considering the high cost of living there. After years of floundering, the hard reality of finances set in. I eventually found myself in the corporate

world, but I was not inspired. To get through the days, I had to put my soul in a cage, where it rarely sang. It wasn't until that middle-of-the-night awakening I described in the introduction that I realized how important it was to live authentically. I did not want to be lying on my death bed with regrets that I did not love people as fully as I should have, or allow my inner artist to reach its potential, or truly see the world around me because stress had blinded me to the beauty of the here and now.

One of the biggest stressors in our lives is our work. I know many people who get stomach aches on Sunday nights just thinking about the next week. Families have been ripped apart due to work stress. When I was in a very stressful job, I used to remind my staff that they needed to put their family and health first. The company is not going to be at their bedside when they die. The people they love and who love them are the ones who will be there. They are the ones who matter, and while I wanted them all to be dedicated and work hard, I did not want to see anyone sacrifice a work-life balance or their health and their relationships for a job. It's simply not worth it.

The word dharma has many meanings attached to it. In Buddhism, it's often used to refer to the teachings of the Buddha. I've heard it used in many other contexts, though, including the path of righteousness, law, duty and vocation. Here, I used dharma to describe vocation in a spiritual context. Your vocation is not just your job. It is your divine calling, and so it is your duty to respond to that call. By answering the call, you are walking the path of righteousness. There is no one else like you in this world and there never will be again. Your gifts were meant to be shared with the world and not put

in a cage to be forgotten. By walking the path of dharma, you allow your soul the expression for which it deeply longs.

Responding to your calling does not mean you have to give up your job and go live in the Himalayas, although you may decide to do just that at some point. Walking the path of dharma might mean changing your perspective of your current situation or simply adding something to your life rather than removing your current line of work. After deep introspection, you may indeed decide to change careers like I did, or at least change your position or company. Whatever you decide, be sure that you are being true to your calling and your authentic self. Rather than listening to the harsh critic of the ego that tells you that you need to have a certain job title or salary to feel good about yourself, listen to the gentle, quiet voice of the soul and be open to its messages. Note any resistance that arises, for it might just be the signpost leading you in the right direction: back to the soul.

Learn to love the work you have

Joshua Rosenthal, founder of the Institute of Integrative Nutrition, advises people to find work they love or learn to love the work they already have. Are there interesting projects you can take on or other positions within the company that suit your skills better? Sometimes, a few tweaks to what we are already doing can make a huge difference. The saying "The grass is greener on the other side of the fence" seems to be truest when it comes to our jobs. Instead of envying another person's job, try seeing your job from another person's perspective or remember a time when someone commented that your job seemed fun, interesting or worthwhile. What did this person envy or admire about it? The feeling of importance due to having people to manage?

Your income? Your lack of responsibility? When I was in lower-level jobs making a low salary, I envied those in position of power who had people to manage, a higher income, and more respect in the company. However, when I became that higher-level manager, I daydreamed about having a lower-level job again, even though that would mean a drastic pay cut, because I remembered the days of having less money but less stress and more time. Time and a peace of mind were two things I gave up to climb the ladder and earn a higher income. Everything comes at a price.

Seeing the Light

Learn to see the light in others. We all have light and shadow, yin and yang. We tend to focus only on the shadow in others, particularly the people we just don't gel with very well, or even a spouse or friend who has been rubbing us the wrong way lately. It can cause even more stress when it is a boss or a co-worker because our current livelihood depends on our survival in the workplace. Perhaps that person's characteristics mimic the characteristics we dislike about ourselves or someone from an earlier period of our lives, and our attack on the other person, be it mental or verbal, is displaced. The reverse may be true for the other person who seems to be attacking us. This is quite common. The next time someone irritates you, be it a co-worker with whom you have tension or your parent who always knows how to say just the right thing to set you off, imagine that person surrounded by beautiful, yellow light, and wish that person healing. Next, ask yourself the following question: "What is a possible positive reason for this person's behavior or my reaction to it?" Don't let up until you have your answer.

For example, your boss, who consistently seems to pick on

every mistake you make, could have several motivations that come from light and shadow. Some shadow reasons could be that he or she has a horrible personal life and is taking it out on you, or is being pressured by his or her boss and is passing that stress on to you, or is a perfectionist who is never happy with anything. It is much easier to see the shadow side, and while it's important to see where the person might be coming from, even if it's negative, it's also important to explore positive possibilities from a perspective of light. Here are some of those possibilities:

A. She sees your potential and is pushing you to reach it.
B. He knows things about the state of the company that you don't, and by pushing you to what seems like perfection, he is actually trying to save his job, your job, and maybe even the company as a whole.
C. She takes pride in her work and wants direct, frequent criticism so that she can do a better job. She is simply making the assumption that you want feedback in the same manner that she does.
D. He is very thick-skinned and simply has no idea how he comes across. His feelings are positive, but he's just not coming across that way.

It still hurts, though, so what is one to do? Combine some of the above techniques as well as techniques from some of the other paths. For example, do one of the pranayamas mentioned in chapter two. You can do them right before work or whatever other stressful situation you are about to encounter. When you see this person, imagine her surrounded by a sphere of light. After all, we are all souls walking around temporarily in a body. Say only positive or neutral things about this person, even if everyone in the staff

room is having fun ranting about her horrible traits.

If your boss or a client storms into your office feeling upset, rather than putting up a defensive barrier, empathize with this person. If someone is angry or frustrated, even if it is directed at you, that person is in pain and deserves some empathy from you. You can show empathy by saying, "I understand you are upset about the situation, and so am I. Here is what I'm doing to rectify it." As soon as the person realizes you are on his or her side, I guarantee that the situation will calm several degrees. This works much better than becoming defensive and using excuses.

When she gives you what you perceive to be negative feedback, practice either Tonglen from chapter two or breathing through your heart while listening in a detached manner to what the person is saying. (I know, it's not easy, but it will become much easier with practice). Look for the light in the comment, no matter how harsh. Even if it's obviously negative and the person has taken it so far as to yell at you or insult you, you can find light. In one of my jobs, I was on the receiving end of an over-stressed, upper-level manager who took his stress out on me in a negative, unprofessional manner. Where was the light in that, you may ask? It reinforced how I did NOT want to treat others and made me analyze how I may have over-reacted to others in the past due to stress. It was also the catalyst for my giving notice at the company where I was no longer happy anyway. The day I gave notice, I was offered a wonderful job with an amazing boss. Silently or verbally thank that person for the lesson, and wish him or her healing.

Find work that loves you

When have you felt appreciated for a skill or talent? Make a list of times you were using your talents in a way you found rewarding. Do you see any patterns? When I was feeling stuck in a well-paying, but high-stress job where I was utilizing my talents but felt unappreciated for them, I started digging deep. I realized that although my Type A characteristics made me good at my job, the type of stress and hectic nature of the job exacerbated the negative characteristics of being a Type A. It brought out aggression in me that carried over to my home life. I read books for inspiration and performed many soul-searching exercises. Nutrition and wellness kept popping up. I didn't want to go into debt for yet another graduate degree, as I already had an MA, but I just put my intentions out there and trusted something would come up. And it did. I started talking to anyone and everyone about my interests. During a conversation with my cousin, she mentioned that I might like to attend the school she was attending in order to become a Certified Integrative Nutrition Coach. When she described the career, my heart did back flips. This was *exactly* what I'd been looking for all of this time. I enrolled at the Institute of Integrative Nutrition, quit my job several months later, and started my own health coaching practice. Every day, I feel incredibly lucky to have the opportunity to do what I am doing. I feel so grateful to the writers of the books I read and to my cousin for sharing the opportunity with me.

Accept yourself for who you are now and not who you used to be or think you should be. I didn't always have a passion for nutrition. For many years, my passion was traveling, learning other languages and studying other cultures. I taught ESL and

loved it. Over the years, my interests have shifted to include health and wellness as I have learned, grown, and widened my net of experiences. Twenty years ago, I couldn't wait to get out of the Midwest to go live in other countries, and I did just that. I loved living overseas. In recent years, I became drawn to the area where I was raised and the surrounding land. Respect who you've become, and understand that everyone is in a constant state of change. What do you love now? What makes you want to get up in the morning? How much of what you love can you incorporate into your current job or lifestyle? If you get knots in your stomach on Sunday nights, you are probably in the wrong career, or at least in the wrong job. Life is too short to have Sundays ruined due to dread of Mondays.

Although we are constantly changing, there are some things about us that remain constant. One of the most helpful exercises I did was to list all of the things I loved doing as a child and find the adult equivalent to those activities or how I could work those activities into a job. Writing came up over and over, but I kept thinking this meant I had to write full-time as a career, and I knew how unprofitable that could be. As I kept searching and probing, I realized I could fit writing into my career as a health coach by blogging and writing newsletters, books and magazine articles in addition to seeing clients.

Examining what you loved as a child is a good signpost for what you should be doing now. Make a list of all of the times you felt joyful and inspired from childhood through adulthood. Highlight key words that describe these activities. Do you see any patterns? What skills did you use? What did you like about these activities? Can you incorporate these into

your current job or change jobs within the same company? Can some of them fit into an entirely different career? Which career(s)? Start talking to anyone and everyone you know about your interests and see what comes up.

Volunteerism

Another way to offer your skills to the world is through volunteering. I know many people who are mostly satisfied with their jobs, but feel a component is missing. Rather than trying to find the "perfect" job, they supplement it by volunteering at a local community-based organization. I used to work for a refugee resettlement organization and loved that line of work. I particularly appreciated the volunteers who helped out in the ESL department. They were compassionate people of all ages and vocational backgrounds. Non-profit organizations offer warm, feel-good environments, and most of the clients are very appreciative of the services they are receiving. It's a great way to sharpen your skills, develop new skills, meet a wonderful group of people, and become more visible in your community. Most importantly, though, you are giving your time, energy and resources to good people who have found themselves in a bad situation. It is much more satisfying to give your time to others and to connect directly with the people you are helping than to send money with a quick click of a button, soon to be forgotten. Giving your time to others can bring immeasurable satisfaction. Pick an organization that fits with the skills, activities, and passions you discovered by doing the activity above. See where the path leads you.

Be a Benedictine Monk

St. Benedict, a Catholic saint, believed in hard, physical labor

and felt the plow was to be revered as much as the chalice. Seeing your chores and your line of work in this light can make them seem less of a drudgery and more of a divine calling. Even nuns and monks don't spend all day praying and meditating. They have assigned chores at the monastery, tend to the sick, serve food in shelters, and provide counseling services to the suffering. Whatever your work, whether it be working in accounts payable or selling a product, find a way to do it from the place of spirit. Each morning as you walk into your office, take a moment to be silent and ask yourself how you can be of service to your company and your clients. How can you best utilize your gifts that day? Each time you change tasks or leave your desk, remind yourself to keep this in mind, to feel grateful, and to breathe.

When you are doing your daily chores, listen to the sound of the water as you are doing the dishes, inhale the earthy scent of the leaves as you rake, and see how completely present you can be. Even if you are doing repetitive tasks at work, listen to the rhythmic sound of your fingers striking the keyboard or the hum of the machine nearby. Repetitive work can be tedious or meditative. Many find knitting to be relaxing because of its repetitive nature. Slow your breathing and feel a sense of gratitude for having a job, even if it doesn't fit your passions, because it is a stepping stone on the path to one that does, even if you can't visualize it yet.

Gently bring your mind back if it starts to wander. Instead of simply bringing it back to your breath, bring it back to both your breath and the activity you are doing. How does it feel, smell, look? What details do you notice that you never noticed before? There are lessons to be learned from the garden hoe, the pot of stew, or the hum of a busy office. If you

are not thinking about what's next and not wanting to hurry to be done with it before you rush off to the next thing on your list, the time won't feel so wasted. In fact, you might look at chores or your line of work as another opportunity for service. You are either providing service to your clients and company, or you are serving your family, your guests, your garden or yourself.

Chapter 7 ~ Walk the Path

1. Make a list of your favorite things and favorite activities as a child. What did you love? What were your dreams? When you played, were you climbing trees, reading fantasy books, having tea parties with stuffed animals, riding your dirt bike, or building things with Legos? These are all hints to pay attention to as you walk the path of dharma.
2. Research a non-profit organization that interests you and call the organization to find out about volunteer opportunities.
3. Make a list of all of the skills you enjoy using in your current job and which ones you don't enjoy. Which skills do you enjoy using that you aren't using in your job? Make an appointment with your boss to find out about possible projects that will allow you to use the skills you love to a greater degree.
4. Do an informational interview with someone who has a job you find interesting.
5. Compliment someone at work every day, and vow to bring light to the room, regardless of what others may bring.
6. Schedule something fun to do at the end of each day to reward yourself for a hard day at work.
7. Go with your gut. As you walk any path, you will only see one small piece of it at a time. Even though you don't know where the end of the path will lead, it will be revealed to you one step at a time. Do you feel drawn to take an art class or to speak to a stranger at a coffee shop? Do it. See where it leads you. You will get much further on the path if you allow the marriage of instinct and spontaneous action. Challenge yourself to do this regularly.

Chapter 8

The Fire Gathering Path ~ Sacred Circle of Relationships and Community

"When you learn to love and let your self be loved, you come home to the hearth of your own spirit." – John O'Donahue, Anam Cara

At the end of a yoga class, the teacher and students say the word "Namaste," which means "I bow to the divine in you." In the Celtic tradition, there is also a recognition of the divinity in others, and strangers are seen as bringers of gifts and illumination. Friendship is sacred, and at the deepest level, a friend aids in our spiritual development. In his book, *Anam Cara,* John O'Donohue defines the meaning of a friend beautifully when he writes, "A friend is a loved one who awakens your life in order to free the wild possibilities within you." Many of us have people we call friends, but it is perhaps only a few rare times in our lives that we connect with others on a deeper, soul level. When we do, we should cherish them, for they help guide us back to the soul, setting us free.

Our family is also part of this sacred circle of friendship and community. This fire-gathering circle is where all of the roads intersect at one point or another, whether it's sharing a pot of steamy homemade stew on a winter's day, walking together along a beach at sunset, gathering in prayer at a temple, mosque or church, running down a soccer field with the wind in your hair as you pass the ball to your teammate, or working on a project with a group to launch a new product that will bring healing, joy or relief to those who consume it. It's why all of the other paths matter. It is through our connection with others that we are able to travel out of the dark valley to return

to the light of the soul. It is not something we do alone, and so we must gather around the fire in celebration of each other.

My grandmother: a love story

I was very close to my grandparents and visited them often. My grandmother on my dad's side lived within walking distance, and as I grew older, I spent more and more time at her house. We would sit over cups of coffee and talk for hours or watch the sunset while sitting on her swing in the yard without saying a word. When I returned from living in England, I brewed a pot of English-style tea for her, and she was hooked. Instead of calling me up to ask me if I'd come down for coffee, she'd ask me for a cup of tea. Many people knew to call me at my grandmother's when they wanted to reach me since I spent more time at her house than anywhere else.

My grandmother was highly evolved on a spiritual level and was one of the kindest people I've ever known. She loved people. We used to joke that there wasn't a wedding or funeral in town that she didn't attend. Wherever people gathered, she'd be there. She laughed easily and often. She loved to tease. She would walk to hell and back for any of her family, and sometimes she did. When she died, I stood by her side as she took her last breath and watched as the light faded from her eyes. The room was full of family who loved her, and as she passed away and for several minutes afterwards, we all commented on how warm the room felt. There was a strange glow that wasn't from the setting sun. It was standing room only at her funeral, and as I left the church, I remember seeing lines of people out the door because the church was too small to hold all of those who wanted to attend. When a soul leaves the body, the only thing that is left is the energy of love.

It is the only thing that matters. No one really dies. Your relationship just changes, and the love you shared remains within and around you always.

Who in your life represents joy and connection for you? What qualities does this person possess that you can strive to develop in yourself? Can you spend more time with this person, learning from his or her wisdom?

The magic penny

We may be tempted to go inwards as we repair the damage of stress and build inner strength to combat it in the future, but our relationships with others play a crucial role in living healthy, happy lives. It's an integral part of the human experience and of our development. When we allow stress to overcome us, we fail to see the people right in front of us and to give our time to the people who matter the most. My grandmother experienced several tragedies in her life, and she spent the last twenty years of it living alone as a widow. She was always cheerful in spite of all of the darkness she had faced, and when asked if she felt lonely living alone, she replied, "I'm alone, but not lonely." She loved others unconditionally, and in turn, she received much love. So lesson number one: If you want more love in your life, then be sure to give it. When you were a child, you may have learned a song about love being like a magic penny. If you hold onto it and don't share it, you won't have anything, but if you "spend it, lend it, you'll have so many it will end up all over the floor."

When is the last time you spent quality time with your loved ones? Sitting in front of the TV or working away at your computer while others are in the room doesn't count. When

did you last have a conversation with your significant other or best friend that went far beyond superficial banter or mundane chatter? How often do you get together with friends and family? Make a point to connect with others daily. Look people in the eyes and listen deeply instead of looking away as you think about what you want to say next. When you ask how they are doing, mean it. Is there a sigh as your neighbor gives the perfunctory reply "I'm fine," in response to your question, "How are you?" If so, ask again and be prepared to listen. Use all of the other practices in this book to listen and be fully present rather than thinking about what you are going to say next.

Find your tribe

Connecting with others who share similar passions and interests is one of the most important things you can do for your health. As I mentioned in the Warrior chapter, we are pack animals at heart, and the stronger our community, the more resilient we are. It is important not only to connect with family and loved ones, but to find your "tribe." Are you deeply spiritual, a nature enthusiast, a raw foods foodie or an artist? Finding others to share these activities with can allow you to grow and connect in amazing ways. It is a great way to let go of everyday worries and just play.

Your tribe can also be a soft spot to land when hardship strikes. People enjoy helping others, but it can be difficult to ask for help. By joining a group, you are also asking for support, as are the others in the group. It can seem less daunting to ask for support in this environment, even if it's about a completely unrelated subject matter. Try joining a couple of local groups where you can meet others with similar interests. My grandmother went to Catholic mass daily and

enjoyed attending the church's Homemaker's Club meetings. I have found community through organizations such as The Art of Living Foundation and my local ice skating club. My other grandparents, who were avid golfers, belonged to the country club and played euchre on certain nights of the week with several of their golf buddies. My sister, who always loved to dance, but found it too difficult to do while raising three children, recently reignited this passion by taking ballroom dancing with her husband. Once a week, they get a babysitter for the kids and go out on their "date." Dancing requires them to look at each other instead of looking around worrying about what the kids are doing. They must also connect through touch and be in tune with each other's rhythm. When they come home, they teach the new steps they learned to their kids, and the kids love it. They have a group of friends who now want them to teach ballroom dancing to them so that they can all go dancing together! Life is so much richer when you pursue your passion with others, celebrate each other's successes, and support each other in times of need. The bonds that develop can last a lifetime.

Mirror Image

When you become angry or irritated with someone, take two seconds to breathe before reacting, and then take an honest look in the mirror. Is this person reflecting something you dislike about yourself or reminding you of something in your past with which you have not fully dealt? Use your irritations as an opportunity for self-examination and growth. It is rare that a disagreement is entirely one person's fault. Our own stories often cloud the lens through which we see a particular situation or person, leading to misperceptions. We draw certain people into our lives because they have lessons to teach

us, even if they are unaware of it. Listen. Learn. Seek out the people who annoy you, and challenge yourself not only to learn something from them, but also to appreciate something about them. When we can learn to appreciate another, the line that divides us from them becomes less definite. We soften, and as we do so, the flower of compassion opens. Merriam Webster's online dictionary defines compassion as "sympathetic consciousness of others' distress combined with a desire to alleviate it." When others anger or irritate us, we tend to put up walls, when instead we should recognize this behavior as a sign of suffering and seek to lend a helping hand. However, this does not mean you must put up with emotional or physical abuse from another. There are times when physically distancing ourselves from another is important for our wellness, but we should strive to do so from a place of compassion. I had a friend who was being physically abused by her husband and had a great deal of rage as a result, which is understandable. She was also very religious, and through her religion, learned to let her anger give way to compassion while taking the necessary legal steps to protect herself from further abuse.

Bury the hatchet

Is there anyone with whom you have unresolved issues? How would you feel if that person died today and you didn't have the chance to find resolution? We assume we will all live to old age, but we don't know when our number is up. I was shocked and saddened to find out how many of my high school classmates have passed away from various causes, and I feel I have another forty plus years of life left in me. In the end, carrying around resentment does no one any good. It depletes your energy and gnaws at your very soul. Even if

you can't resolve the issue, agree to disagree and let it go. None of us truly know how long we have in this world.

Right Speech

This is another great Buddhist teaching that can be used as an active meditation. Rather than sitting on a cushion and being still, you can incorporate right speech into everyday activities. What we say and how we say it affects our neural pathways, reinforcing them for good or ill. Gossip may feel good on the superficial level of gratification, but it does not bring us deep joy, peace or satisfaction. If anything, it brings disturbance to our inner calm, churning ourselves inside. In the end, the negativity you put out into the world comes back to you even stronger, like a boomerang. In other words, "You reap what you sow." Be careful with your words, for your words are seeds that become your harvest. When you find yourself about to say something negative about another person or directed at another person, take a couple of seconds to breathe deeply and slowly before moving forward. Will having this conversation help you resolve the issue? Maybe. Sometimes, other people can provide an alternative perspective that allows us to perceive someone else in a more positive light. But if this is just an opportunity to rant, your words are better left unspoken, and those two seconds could save you, and the other person, unnecessary energy and heartache.

Chapter 8 ~ Walk the Path

1. Join an existing group, expand your current group, or start your own group that will allow you to explore at least one of your passions with others. Meet with this group regularly.
2. Call a friend or relative you haven't spoken to in months or years.
3. Make it a goal to meet one new person per week and to stay in contact.
4. Make a list of unresolved issues you have with the loved ones in your life, and then make a plan to resolve these issues once and for all, or at least to start the process.
5. Invite friends and family to your home for a potluck dinner with a theme, such as your favorite food from childhood or a dish from your favorite holiday.
6. For a week, focus on saying one nice thing to everyone you speak to each day. What changes do you notice in your relationships?
7. Make a list of 5 people who bring out the best in you and/or the 5 people you would want at your side when you die. Vow to spend a majority of your time with these people.

Conclusion

All of these paths really form one large path that continuously leads us back to soul, our origin, our eternal authentic self. Returning to the light of soul and tapping into its unique rhythm is a conscious choice that must be made every moment of the day, which is difficult to do under the glaring lights and chaotic noise of modernization. The activities in this book will help you as you practice being more present in all areas of your life and strive to maintain balance. Balance and consciousness allow your soul to break through the mists that would normally obscure it. By paying attention, you can sense your soul that, like a lighthouse, will guide you through the obscure, choppy waters to creativity and freedom.

Don't try to make all of these changes at once, for that will surely take you off the path and onto the rocky road of frustration. Instead, use your intuition to pick a few tips to try, and do them until they become habit. For example, for one week, you could focus on your breathing throughout the day and take a nature walk during your lunch hour. Another week, you could do the above, but add a tip from the restoration chapter and eat your meals in a calm, reflective space. How you integrate the paths is up to you, but diligent practice and integration are key to rebalancing your mind, body and spirit in order to find freedom, fulfillment and inspiration. Be sure to re-read the chapters. As you evolve and develop a level of automaticity in some areas, other parts of the book that you forgot about or never noticed will start to gleam, beckoning you to pay attention.

Although time will slowly etch its story across your face and your body will weaken as it passes through the years, the timeless essence within will always be there: an untouched fountain of eternal youth. Whether or not you believe you have a soul, or that it will or will not reincarnate, you will never have another life like this one. Never again will you appear in this specific form at this moment in time, so consider each day a blessing, including the harsh lessons it sometimes brings. After all, the sun still rises after the darkest nights, and the flowers still bloom after the coldest of winters. Find something, anything, to appreciate each day about yourself and the life you are living.

As I finish this book, the snow is falling gently, lightly dusting the birch trees and evergreens outside my window. In spite of the below-freezing temperatures this winter, I often still heard birds singing in the morning as I stepped out to inhale some fresh, non-heated air. Their song reminds me of the circular nature of life. Although it's hard to believe spring will ever come when the sun hasn't made an appearance in days, and the air is so cold it hurts to breathe it, the birds remind me that all will come full circle. I will enjoy the fire in the fireplace a bit longer and use the time indoors to read, reflect and learn, so that in the spring, I will blossom fully as the buds unfurl to become leaves. When you are so overwhelmed you can do nothing else, step out into nature and just breathe.

Works Cited

Chapter 1:

Bates, Brian. *The Way of Wyrd: Tales of an Anglo-Saxon Sorcerer.* Carlsbad: Hay House, 2005. Print.

Bruton-Seal, Julie and Matthew Seal. "Birch Trees: Natural Medicine in Your Backyard." *Mother Earth News: The Original Guide to Living Wisely.* 24 Jan. 2014. Web. March 28, 2015.

Brydon, Bill. *A Walk in the Woods: Rediscovering America on the Appalachian Trail.* New York: Broadway Books, 1998. Print.

Cymraes, Winter. "Tree Lore: Birch." *The Order of Bards, Ovates & Druids.* Web. March 28, 2015.

Greer, John Michael. *The Druidry Handbook: Spiritual Practice Rooted in the Living Earth.* San Francisco: Red Wheel/Weiser, LLC, 2006. Print.

Maloof, Jean. "Old Growth Air." *The Order of Bards, Ovates & Druids.* Web. March 28, 2015.

Pollan, Michael. "The Intelligent Plant." *The New Yorker.* The New Yorker mag., 23 Dec. 2013. Web. January 5, 2015.

Richard, Michael Graham. "Best Air-Filtering Houseplants, According to NASA." *Mother Nature Network.* 30 Nov. 2012. Web. March 28, 2015.

Chapter 2:

Chodron, Pema. *Start Where You Are: A Guide to Compassionate Living.* Boston: Shambhala Publications, 1994. Print.

McAlister, Michael. Infinite Smile Sangha. Lafayette Christian Church, Lafayette, CA. Various dates, 2014. Dharma talks.

Wuttke, Marty. Center for Spiritual Enlightenment. Center for Spiritual Enlightenment, San Jose, CA. 17 January, 2007. Presentation on meditation and the brain.

Wuttke, Marty. *The Wuttke Institute.* Web. March 28, 2015.

Shankar, Ravi. *Upanishads.* Art of Living Foundation. Art of Living Center, Los Angeles, CA. 20 – 22 April, 2012. Discourse on the Upanishads.

Chapter 3:

Cameron, Julia. *The Artist's Way: A Spiritual Path to Higher Creativity.* New York: Jeremy P Tarcher/Putnam, 1992. Print.

Wordsworth, William. *The Prelude.* New York: Holt, Rinehart and Winston, 1964.

Chapter 4:

"The Dangers of Painkillers: A Special Report." *Consumer Reports.* Consumer Reports mag, September 2014. Web. March 28, 2015.

Lad, Vasant. *The Complete Book of Ayurvedic Home Remedies.* New York: Three Rivers Press, 1998.

Learn.Genetics: Genetics Science Learning Center. University of Utah Health Sciences. Web. March 28, 2015.

Therapeutic Research Faculty, Natural Medicine's

Comprehensive Database Consumer's Version. *Medline Plus.* U.S. National Library of Medicine National Institutes of Health. Web. March 28, 2015.

Chapter 5:

Hyman, Mark. "Food Bites with Dr.Hyman – What can I do to stay asleep and sleep more deeply?" *DrHyman.com.* 8 Feb. 2015. Web. March 28, 2015.

Chapter 6:

Yogananda, Paramhansa. *Autobiography of a Yogi.* New York: The Philosophical Library, 1946.

Chapter 8:

O'Donohue, John. *Anam Cara: A Book of Celtic Wisdom*. New York: Harper Collins, 1997.

Merriam-Webster.com. Web. March 29, 2015.

A Review of *Soul Destination*

Jennifer has a unique and enthusiastic attitude toward wellness that can be seen in her book. I highly recommend reading it.

She actually makes taking care of yourself -- body, mind, and spirit -- sound interesting and doable. Heck, she even talked me into taking up ice skating at the age of 49 because it would be fun and a great way for me to exercise. And you know what, she was right!

~ Dr. Shelley Coughlin, D.C., Coughlin Chiropractic

About the Author

Jennifer Malins is a certified Integrative Nutrition Coach, writer and teacher. She received her integrative nutrition coach certification through the Institute of Integrative Nutrition in New York City. She is also a licensed HeartMath® coach through the Institute of HeartMath®, a credentialed teacher, and holds an MA in English Literary Studies from the University of Durham, United Kingdom. She has written numerous newspaper and magazine articles, has appeared on local TV, leads workshops, and sees clients for one-to-one health coaching. She currently writes for Classical Music Indy's *Note* magazine. Jennifer also loves writing fiction. Currently, she is working on a novel. In addition to writing and nutrition, Jennifer loves ice skating, yoga, taking long nature walks, experimenting in the kitchen, playing various musical instruments, and spending time with family. She lives in Indianapolis with her husband and dog.

Back cover author photo by Morgan Bradley.